Twayne's United States Authors Series

EDITOR OF THIS VOLUME

Lewis Leary

*University of North Carolina
Chapel Hill*

J. H. Ingraham

TUSAS 361

From the frontispiece to Ingraham's *Santa Claus* (Boston: H. L. Williams, 1844).

J. H. Ingraham

J. H. INGRAHAM

By ROBERT W. WEATHERSBY, II

Dalton Junior College

TWAYNE PUBLISHERS

A DIVISION OF G. K. HALL & CO., BOSTON

Copyright © 1980 by G. K. Hall & Co.

Published in 1980 by Twayne Publishers,
A Division of G. K. Hall & Co.
All Rights Reserved

Printed on permanent/durable acid-free paper and bound
in the United States of America

First Printing

Library of Congress Cataloging in Publication Data

Weathersby, Robert W., II
J. H. Ingraham.

(Twayne's United States authors series ; TUSAS 361)
Bibliography: p. 147 - 159
Includes index.
1. Ingraham, Joseph Holt, 1809-1860. 2. Novelists,
American — 19th century — Biography.   3.   Protestant
Episcopal Church in the U.S.A. — Clergy — Biography.
4.   Clergy — United States — Biography.
PS2048.I52Z94   813'.3 [B]   80-16555
ISBN 0-8057-7302-9

For Dorothy

Contents

About the Author
Preface
Acknowledgments
Chronology
1. The Professor and the Author   15
2. The Minister   33
3. The Beginnings with Harper & Brothers   49
4. Five Years and Eighty Novels   71
5. Periodical Productions   92
6. The Minister's Literary Products   113
7. Epilogue   132
   Notes and References   135
   Selected Bibliography   147
   Index   160

About the Author

Dr. Robert W. Weathersby, II, a native of Tennessee, is Assistant Professor of English and Administrator of the Regents' Testing Program at Dalton Junior College in Dalton, Georgia. He holds his B.A. and M.A. degrees from George Peabody College for Teachers; his Ph.D. is from the University of Tennessee in Knoxville where he was awarded the Durant da Ponte Dissertation Fellowship in American Literature. An active participant in several professional organizations, he is a contributing abstracter for *Abstracts of English Studies,* has contributed articles to various professional journals and reference works, and is editor of the forthcoming *Lafitte: The Pirate of the Gulf* by J. H. Ingraham.

Preface

The name of Joseph Holt Ingraham (1809-1860) is not a familiar one to most students of American literature. Though Ingraham wrote some of the best-selling novels of the nineteenth century, and though in his lifetime he outsold the better-known authors who published from 1835 to 1860, Ingraham is so little regarded today as to be forgotten by all but the smallest number of readers. Lack of familiarity with Ingraham's life and works is a main cause of this neglect; Ingraham, unwittingly, contributed to his own obscurity by leaving little record of his life. His voluminous production of over one hundred novels and another hundred tales, sketches, and poems contributed to the various newspapers, periodicals, and annuals of the 1830s, 1840s, and 1850s, adds to the reluctance of many readers to evaluate his works. Not many people, therefore, have studied Ingraham because his output was so large, and most of those who have surveyed his writings have read the same two or three novels and disagreed on the facts of his life.

A critical introduction to Ingraham's life and works will fill in some of the gaps in knowledge and determine whether the obscurity of this prolific author is merited. Though Ingraham was so tremendously productive, he apparently left no journals or diaries, other than the parish reports he filed in his later years as a minister, that would aid the modern biographer; but some fifty extant letters help in charting his movements as well as in giving a few glimpses into his private life. Apparently Ingraham was as damned by dollars as was Herman Melville, for his letters and notes often indicate the precarious financial condition of the writer who contended in a mid-nineteenth-century market still dominated by English authors and handicapped by the lack of a firm copyright law.

All of the known fictional works by Ingraham have been read in the preparation of this study. Jacob Blanck's listing of Ingraham's works in his *Bibliography of American Literature,* vol. 4 (1963), is followed, though several novels he lists as unlocated have been discovered and are added to this study. To come to grips with the problems that a study of Ingraham presents, more than thirty surviving newspapers have been examined from the Maine, Mississippi, Alabama, and Tennessee towns in which Ingraham lived or with which he was associated.

Ingraham's forgotten periodical publications have also been consulted in an effort to arrive at a well-rounded, informed estimate of his work. No definitive listing of Ingraham's periodical contributions exists, but a thorough combing of the files of Ingraham-era publications has resulted in the most complete list to date of those publications. The results of this search are presented in Chapter 5.

Because the facts of Ingraham's life have often been in doubt, misreported, or simply unknown, and because a definitive biography of the man has yet to be written, it seemed appropriate to delineate all that is known about Ingraham's life and the strictures under which he wrote for publication. Although the first and second chapters indicate as much as is known about Ingraham, there are gaps that may never be filled. Little can be documented about Ingraham's life before 1830, but the picture becomes clearer after that date.

Chapter 3 covers the years from 1835 through 1841, when Harper & Brothers published Ingraham's work. Chapter 4 deals with the years Ingraham catered most to popular tastes, the years his novels were published in cheap, paperback editions. The novels resulting from his ministry are treated in chapter 6, and an estimate of Ingraham's place in letters occupies the final chapter.

Because Ingraham's work is so unfamiliar to the average reader, it has been thought appropriate to summarize more of his work than would be necessary in a study of a more familiar author. Such summaries illustrate the range and subject matter of his work as well as give the reader unfamiliar with Ingraham some basis on which to judge critical comments upon them. Secondary source commentaries on Ingraham's writings are most often those of contemporary reviewers who first hailed his work, then grew disappointed, and finally ignored him during the period of his greatest productivity. Twentieth-century critics have paid him scant attention.

Joseph Holt Ingraham deserves a hearing, and it is the purpose

Preface

of this study to give him that chance. He may never again enjoy the popularity he once did, but students of the novel and of antebellum civilization will almost certainly note that Ingraham and his work deserve more than the almost total oblivion that they now inhabit.

I acknowledge with pleasure the people who have contributed to this study. Professor Richard Beale Davis offered continual encouragement. F. DeWolfe Miller, Edward W. Bratton, Mark A. Christiansen, and Robert A. Dedmon contributed constructive criticism. Mrs. Beulah Hagan of Harper & Row provided early Ingraham book contracts, while Mrs. R. L. Wyatt helpfully supplied pertinent parish records from Holly Springs, Mississippi. Nash Burger suggested several ideas as did Warren French. Ron McBride and Steve Cox redrew and photographed the portrait of Ingraham.

Librarians at the following institutions aided me in numerous ways: American Antiquarian Society, Haverford College, Historical Society of Pennsylvania, Maine Historical Society, Massachusetts Historical Society, Mississippi Department of Archives and History, New York Public Library, Pierpont Morgan Library, Portland Public Library, United States National Archives and Records Service, University of the South, University of Tennessee, University of Virginia, and Yale University.

I owe my greatest debt to my wife Dorothy who proofread, edited, typed, sacrificed, endured, and loved through the whole long process. This book is for her.

While I acknowledge with gratitude the help of many people, I must also note that any inaccuracies or deficiencies this study may contain are solely my responsibility.

ROBERT W. WEATHERSBY, II

Dalton Junior College
Dalton, Georgia

Acknowledgments

Grateful acknowledgment is made to the following institutions that allowed publication of parts of Ingraham manuscripts: to the Ingraham Collection, Barrett Library, University of Virginia Library for permission to quote from one letter; to the Beinecke Rare Book and Manuscript Library of Yale University for permission to quote from two letters; to the Trustees of the Boston Public Library for permission to quote from two letters; to the Historical Society of Pennsylvania for permission to quote from two letters; to the New York Public Library for permission to quote from one letter in their collection of Joseph Holt Ingraham (Miscellaneous Papers),
>Manuscripts and Archives Division
>The New York Public Library
>Astor, Lenox and Tilden Foundations;

to Harper & Row for permission to quote from three book contracts; to the Massachusetts Historical Society for permission to quote from two letters; and to Haverford College for permission to quote from one letter. I wish also to thank the *Tennessee Historical Quarterly* for permission to quote from my essay, "J. H. Ingraham and Tennessee: A Record of Social and Literary Contributions," which appeared in the Fall, 1975, issue.

Chronology

- 1809 Joseph Holt Ingraham born January 26, in Portland, Maine.
- 1826 Supposedly leaves Maine for South America.
- 1828– Attends Yale College.
- 1829
- 1830 Travels to Natchez, Mississippi; forms a connection with Jefferson College in nearby Washington, Mississippi.
- 1832 May 24, marries Mary Brookes.
- 1833 Publishes his first work, travel sketches, in the *Natchez Courier*.
- 1834 Birth of Laura Caroline Ingraham, his first child.
- 1835 Publishes the travel sketches, with additions, as *The South-West*.
- 1836 *Lafitte,* his first novel.
- 1838 *Burton.* Death of Laura Ingraham.
- 1839 *Captain Kyd* and *The American Lounger.*
- 1841 *The Quadroone.*
- 1842 *The Dancing Feather,* which inaugurates his prolific years as a producer of paperback novels. Goes bankrupt.
- 1843 Begins his association with the publishing firm of the Williams Brothers. Publishes at least eight novels. Son, Prentiss, born.
- 1844 Publishes at least nineteen novels.
- 1845 Publishes at least twenty-five novels.
- 1846 Publishes at least sixteen novels.
- 1847 Publishes at least ten novels. Is confirmed to study for the ministry in the Protestant Episcopal Church and moves to Nashville, Tennessee.
- 1850 Begins serialization of "Letters from Adina."
- 1851 Ordained a deacon; assigned to a missionary post in Aberdeen, Mississippi.
- 1852 Ordained to the priesthood.
- 1853 Transfers to St. John's Church in Mobile, Alabama.

1855 Publishes "Letters from Adina" as *The Prince of the House of David,* his best-selling and most famous work.
1857 Resigns his Mobile parish; accepts a church in Riverside, Tennessee.
1858 Leaves Riverside; accepts a charge in Holly Springs, Mississippi.
1859 Publishes *The Pillar of Fire.* Receives honorary LL.D. from the University of Mississippi.
1860 Publishes *The Throne of David* and *The Sunny South.* Accidentally shoots himself on December 9 and dies on December 18.

CHAPTER 1

The Professor and the Author

I *The Road to a Vocation*

BORN into a prominent Portland, Maine, family on January 26, 1809, Joseph Holt Ingraham, Jr., seemed destined to become a merchant. His grandfather, the elder Joseph Holt Ingraham (1752-1841), had come to Portland (then called Falmouth and still part of Massachusetts) at age sixteen and become a silversmith. But in his later years the elder Ingraham became a prosperous merchant, shipowner, landowner, and civic leader. A second generation American of English ancestry, he helped his family acquire firm roots in the Maine soil. Extant city directories for Portland beginning in 1823 note that many bearers of the Ingraham name made that city their home.[1] The elder J. H. Ingraham, one of the seven children of his father Edward and his mother Lydia Holt,[2] eventually remarried twice, but records do not reveal how many children he sired. One of his sons, James Milk Ingraham, was the father of Joseph Holt Ingraham, Jr.,[3] who was named after his grandfather J. H. Ingraham.

Very little is known about James M. Ingraham except that he followed in his father's footsteps and also became a merchant. The *Portland Gazette, and Maine Advertiser* for August 25, 1806,[4] notes that James operated a store selling English and West India goods and groceries on Ingraham's Wharf and that he had just taken John Gould into partnership with him. The merchants were in "constant attendance from sun rise till nine o'clock in the evening." In the year of his son's birth, the paper also noted that James kept his counting room (his accounts office) in his store on the family-owned wharf.[5] By 1818, Edward and William Ingraham were running the store, and John Gould was dead.[6] Sometime during the interim, James and his wife Elizabeth

15

Thurston moved their family up the Kennebec River to Hallowell, Maine.

By 1822, James was popular enough in Hallowell to be elected to a committee to seek a postmaster for the town.[7] He seems to have remained in Hallowell until around 1841, when he returned to Portland where he lived until after 1852.[8] He died in Biddeford, south of Portland, on June 3, 1856.[9]

James' son, Joseph Holt Ingraham, Jr., loved the river valleys of the Kennebec and was later to make its banks the setting for several of his stories. Here he grew to young manhood, and here he attended Hallowell Academy "and probably was fitted for college there."[10] It is also apparent that he read widely in his youth, for his later writings display an acquaintance with many of the classics and many of the currently popular English romantics, particularly Scott and Byron.

Sometime before young Ingraham started college, probably in 1826, when he was seventeen, he apparently decided to ship on board one of his grandfather's commercial vessels. Such a project was his first effort toward a possible vocation. He supposedly went to Buenos Aires, Argentina, to become a clerk in a mercantile house, and, while there, "is said to have taken part in a native revolution."[11] No record explains satisfactorily what Ingraham did or did not do in South America, but his 1847 two-part novel, *Paul Perril*, tells the tale of a seventeen-year-old merchant's son who goes to Montevideo, Uruguay, and Buenos Aires to clerk in a mercantile house and ends up getting embroiled in the current revolution.

While it remains unknown how much autobiography there is in *Paul Perril*, the novel appears to be at least semiautobiographical. It is different from most other Ingraham novels; it is one of the very few tales he wrote without a love story; its emphasis is on the "facts" of the adventures of four young men; and its hero, like Ingraham, had a dark complexion, black hair, and black eyes. Though the tale has much to suggest that it is founded in fact, no concrete proof of Ingraham's activities are available until 1828, by which time Ingraham had returned home, seemed to have decided against trying the mercantile business for his vocation, and had decided to attend college.

Ingraham attended Yale College, entering in the latter part of 1828. He wrote, on June 29, 1828, to the Reverend Jeremiah Day, then president of Yale, that he was studying his Latin

The Professor and the Author 17

diligently and expected to "enter on the next commencement." He asks Day "what advantages—or opportunities" there would be "for taking a school occasionally throughout the collegiate course—if a Student should be so inclined?"[12] His interest in teaching school between terms, a common practice in those days, sounds the first note of a recurrent Ingraham theme—that he did not have the means to pay for something (here his college education) without earning it himself. That he was thinking of teaching is another forecast of things to come.

Ingraham attended Yale for only one year. He left for reasons not at present known, but since his grades were satisfactory, he must have been dismissed for personal misconduct. He was given a letter of "dismission" which meant that he might later return to Yale if he chose or even attend another university.[13] That Ingraham next intended to enter Dartmouth College is made clear by another letter to President Day written February 21, 1830, from Hanover, New Hampshire. Besides noting his intention, Ingraham also indicates that he was not a model student at Yale. He writes:

Hon'd Sir—

Some days since. I—wrote you. respecting a renewal of my certificate of dismission—but having received no answer as yet—I presume the letter has not reached you—therefore I will—once more take the liberty to address you upon the subject—and with the supposition. that you have not received it.

You are probably aware of my conduct at New Haven I will not attempt to exculpate myself. On leaving there. I went South and took a School. While engaged therein. I experienced a change of heart—and returning home in the fall [1829] on account of ill health—I, through grace, united myself to the church of christ in Portland—of which Rev Dr Bennet Tyler is Pastor.—

Influenced by my own wishes—and those of my friends. I have concluded to unite myself with some institution—to resume my studies—with the intention of preparing for the ministry of Christ.— For this purpose thro' the medium of Dr. Tyler. I shall apply this week for admission as a beneficiary into Dartmouth college.—but before I can be admitted—it will be nescessary that I shall have my certificate of dismission from Yale. but this I have lost. and that I might obtain a renewal of it. I wrote you 10 or 12 days since—stating the purpose of what I now state—but I had received no answer Thursday last—when I left home for this place.—therefore I have once more taken the liberty to write you on the subject. Are you—willing sir. to give me a renewal of the certificate?—It is true I do not deserve it—I did not deserve to have the certificate when I left college—and had you then been aware of my conduct—you would certainly—not only—have refused it—but would have been perfectly justified in sending me away in disgrace.— Whether to grant or to refuse Sir—I leave entirely to yourself.—I do not deserve it—but I cannot be admitted here—without it. Whether you comply with my wishes or not Sir—will you immediately on the receipt of this send me answer—as shall be waiting here on expense, till I hear from you. If you refuse it sir—I cannot complaine[.] If you comply—I can but thank you—

Respectfully your Obt Servt
Jos. H. Ingraham Jr.[14]

Whether Ingraham received the certificate he requested is not known, but he never matriculated at Dartmouth.[15] It would be interesting to know what his transgression was since he begins several stories on college campuses and has their characters get into a variety of scrapes; but it is even more interesting to note that Ingraham was thinking of becoming a minister seventeen years before he finally settled on that vocation. In that seventeen-year period he became first a teacher and then a famous novelist.

II *Vocation Found*

Ingraham left New England and headed south in the fall of 1830.[16] He went south by ship past Bermuda and the Bahamas to Cuba; from here he proceeded to New Orleans. After a few weeks in New Orleans, he boarded a steamer for Natchez, Mississippi, and, while there, visited several inland Mississippi towns. He was immediately taken with the old Southwest and decided to stay in Natchez. Some critics believe that Ingraham tried law and then had some experience in business before he finally joined the faculty of Jefferson College, which was six miles from Natchez in nearby Washington, Mississippi.[17] From 1830 on, Ingraham was often called "Professor," a title that appeared on many of his later novels.

That Ingraham did teach languages at struggling Jefferson College has never been definitely proved. Records of the now defunct institution do not list him as a faculty member, but contemporary references to his tenure there make it clear that he did have some connection with the school.[18] (It is possible that

Jefferson College is the Southern school referred to by Ingraham in his 1830 letter to Reverend Mr. Day of Yale requesting a renewal of his certificate of dismission.) Benjamin L. C. Wailes, a prominent native of Washington, knew Ingraham intimately and noted that he had heard Ingraham "preach from time to time in the chapel" of the college.[19] *The Natchez* newspaper listed, on November 13, 1830, [20] the full professors at the college, but, under the heading "Assistant Professors and Instructors," it listed only the courses taught, among which were French, Spanish, and English—all subjects Ingraham knew and did teach at other schools in later years. Ingraham, at age twenty-one, could hardly have been a full professor and thus listed in *The Natchez*. Despite these comments by his contemporaries, the case for his teaching at Jefferson College will remain circumstantial until more explicit proof is found.

It is certain, however, that Ingraham did meet his future wife in Washington, Mississippi. He married Mary Elizabeth Odlin Brookes, the daughter of a deceased local planter, on May 24, 1832.[21] Ingraham and his bride seemed to have lived at the Brookes family plantation, Rose Cottage,[22] and though he and his family were to travel a great deal after he began publishing his various works, they would often return to the plantation in Washington; an 1836 story, "Spheeksphobia," was dated from Rose Cottage as was his last published book, *The Sunny South* (1860).

Ingraham also found something else in Mississippi—the materials for the beginning of his career as a writer. His first published material appeared in the *Natchez Courier: and Adams, Jefferson and Franklin Advertiser* on August 23, 1833.[23] This work was the first of a series of "Letters from Louisiana and Mississippi By a Yankee" which ran in the *Natchez Courier* (later the *Courier and Journal*) from 1833 until sometime in 1835. The first eleven "Letters" were published from August 23, 1833, until December 20, 1833. The next letters that are extant appear in the *Courier and Journal* for January 2, 9, and 16, 1835. These "Letters" were published, with minimal changes, as Ingraham's first book, *The South-West*, in 1835. Volume 1 of *The South-West* contains twenty-three chapters; the eleven surviving "Letters" published in the *Natchez Courier* appear as chapters 5 through 15. Twelve "Letters" are lost in 1834 until the series surfaces again in January, 1835, in the *Courier and Journal* with what would become letters 5 through 7 of volume 2 of *The South-West*. Thirteen later letters, then, are not extant, if indeed they were all published in the newspaper.

The letters in the newspaper were addressed to "Friend W.—" and signed "I." "Friend W.—" was almost certainly Ingraham's Washington friend Benjamin L. C. Wailes; *The South-West*, which was published by Harper & Brothers, gives the initials of neither the writer nor the recipient. *The South-West* tells of Ingraham's trip south from New England and his subsequent arrival at Natchez. With Timothy Flint's *Recollections of the Last Ten Years* (1826), it provides a detailed picture of life in New Orleans and Mississippi in the early part of the nineteenth century.

In addition to reflecting life in the old Southwest, the Ingraham volume previews many of the romantic notions and stylistic characteristics that would recur in his later fiction. There was little Ingraham did not like about the romantic South as he saw it. One critic believes that the "longing of the south, for any alien and distant setting, is typical of romanticism, and reflects the effort of . . . . [the writer's] imagination to break away from the fetters of homely experience."[24]

Ingraham received three hundred dollars from Harper's for *The South-West*, the smallest payment he was to receive for any of the books that the New York firm would later publish.[25] *The South-West*, like other travel books in this era, generally sold well. Edgar Allan Poe, who assumed the editorship of the *Southern Literary Messenger*, spoke well of *The South-West* in its review columns.[26] *The South-West*, along with other works published in 1835—William Gilmore Simms' *The Yemassee* and *The Partisan*, John Pendleton Kennedy's *Horse-Shoe Robinson*, Augustus Baldwin Longstreet's *Georgia Scenes*, and Poe's "Berenice" and "Morella"—helped make 1835 a good year for Southern writing, the "annus mirabilis" of the nineteenth century one writer believes.[27]

Ingraham entered the literary world at a time when American authorship had begun "to assume the aspect of a business."[28] He entered in good company, and he entered with a form of book that was "the first genre to be successfully established on a profitable professional basis. It had tremendous social prestige because it was useful and educational, and because its methods were in accord with the reigning Scottish common-sense philosophy, which celebrated actuality."[29] James Harper, of Harper & Brothers, noted that " 'Travels sell about the best of anything we get ahold of. . . . They don't always go with a rush, like a novel . . . but they sell longer, and in the end, pay better.' "[30]

Ingraham had found his vocation. He seemed to accept the terms of professional writing as another author would later state them. It "provides a living for the author, like any other job; . . . it is a main and prolonged, rather than intermittent or sporadic, resource for the writer; . . . it is produced with the hope of extended sale in the open market, like any article of commerce; and . . . it is written with reference to buyers' tastes and reading habits."[31]

After Ingraham "began writing, he did not reside continuously in the South."[32] He was on his way to Portland in July, 1835,[33] and he dated his introduction to *The South-West* from New York in September. His second book and first novel, *Lafitte: The Pirate of the Gulf*, contained a preface written in New York in June of 1836.

Lafitte, dedicated to a fellow Portland native, Henry Wadsworth Longfellow, was an immediate success both critically and financially. Harper & Brothers paid him $1,350 for the two-volume historical romance, and Edgar Allan Poe, in a penetrating review for the *Southern Literary Messenger*, found more to praise than to censure.[34] Ingraham's Lafitte is an intensely Byronic character, and one critic claims that "no novelist before Ingraham had given a Byronic turn to the American historical romance."[35]

Fusion of fact with fiction became another Ingraham staple. Ingraham seemed very much aware that history, "in one form or another, was the chief substance of most successful writing before 1850."[36] An additional mark of *Lafitte*'s success was that the novel was dramatized in August, 1836, for the Bowery Theatre in New York by Miss Louisa Honor de Medina.[37] Medina transformed a number of popular novels into dramas, but few examples of her work survive. Though her dramatization of *Lafitte* is numbered among the lost, her drama must have been popular, for the play went on to Philadelphia in the same year. At least three other Ingraham novels, two of them dealing with pirates, would be dramatized.

Ingraham published his first short story, "The Village Prize," a legend of George Washington, in *The Portland Sketch Book* in 1836. The *Sketch Book* was composed entirely of contributions by then eminent Portland-born writers. Ingraham's inclusion in such company as Henry Wadsworth Longfellow, John Neal, and N. P. Willis after only a little more than a year on the literary scene was an indication of his rising popularity.

On September 29, 1836, Ingraham received an advance of three hundred dollars for his next novel, to be entitled "The Conspirator, or Treason Unveiled," and promised to deliver the manuscript by January 1, 1837.[38] The manuscript was in Harper hands by June 1, 1837,[39] but the financial panic that hit the country in 1837 was almost certainly one of the factors that delayed until 1838 the publication of "The Conspirator," renamed *Burton; or, The Seiges. A Romance.*

Speculation in public lands was one of the reasons that, on May 10, 1837, the New York banks suspended specie payments, "precipitating one of the country's worst financial panics."[40] Book publishers felt the crunch. One critic believes that the panic of 1837 produced a hiatus in the novel-writing career of "almost every writer and publisher of serious fiction in the nation in the 1840's." The two-volume novels that Ingraham was writing were casualties, and Harpers would publish only two more Ingraham tales after *Burton.* Another writer hit by the panic was Poe, who published *The Narrative of Arthur Gordon Pym* in 1838; he wrote no more novels and "died before the native novel found a profitable market." John Pendleton Kennedy was another casualty of the panic, and the South lost a promising writer when he abandoned the profession in disgust after the 1838 publication of his *Rob of the Bowl.*[41]

The first edition of *Burton,* in spite of the country's financial troubles, sold out its three thousand copies in a week.[42] The public interest in the novel, an absorbing account of the early career of Aaron Burr, may have been intensified by Burr's recent death in 1836. Ingraham's interest in Burr might also have been stimulated by the fact that Burr was tried for treason under some oak trees on the Jefferson College campus.[43]

Ingraham sold no fewer than twelve different pieces to periodicals in 1838, and they, no doubt, helped fill in his income of only $750 from *Burton.* The novel deservedly received good reviews, but an editor of the *Portland Transcript* was miffed because the home state paper received no complimentary copy of the work, and he was moved to comment: "Strange that no notice has been taken of this work in the place of the author's nativity—and yet when editors have to purchase works of this kind it is not so very strange. We cannot be expected to purchase and puff at the same time."[44] Longfellow, in what may be termed a fit of professional jealousy, wrote to George W. Greene on October 22 that "A new American novelist has arisen; his name is Professor Ingraham. He is author of The Pirate of the Gulf,— dedicated to me, but without permission,—and the Sieges. He is tremendous—really tremendous. I think he [Ingraham] may say that he writes the worst novels ever written by anybody. But they sell; he gets twelve hundred dollars apiece."[45] Longfellow's works had not yet received that much attention.

By October 16, 1838, Ingraham was back in New York to sign a contract with Harpers for the publication of *Captain Kyd: or The Wizard of the Sea* for which he was paid twelve hundred dollars.[46] *Kyd*, published in 1839, contained a preface dated in January from Natchez where he probably put the finishing touches on the novel. His third Harper novel returned to the sea, ships, and pirates—a combination calculated to draw readers. *Kyd*, dramatized by Joseph Stevens Jones, is one of the two extant dramas based on Ingraham novels. The play is basically a truncation of the Professor's work, often employing the same dialogue; Jones leaves in as much action as possible and omits the descriptions that could not have been transferred easily anyway. The play was produced in Boston in 1839, revived in 1840, 1848, 1850, and 1859; Purdy's National Theatre presented it to New York in 1856.[47] There is no record of Ingraham's having received any royalties from the use of his work.

Ingraham's most successful year for periodical publications was 1839. At least nineteen pieces appeared in various magazine outlets. *The Ladies' Companion* announced in February that it had bought nineteen Ingraham articles which would appear over the next two years.[48] *The Ladies' Companion* was one of the Professor's best periodical customers; it bought from Ingraham thirty-five different titles which appeared in fifty-seven of the seventy monthly issues from January, 1839, through October, 1844, the last issue of the magazine.

Ingraham seems to have traveled a great deal in 1839. After dating his *Kyd* preface from Natchez in January, he appeared in New York on January 17 to sell the Harpers the rights to his next novel, *The Quadroone*,[49] which would not appear in the United States until 1841. He wrote Edward Carey of *Godey's Lady's Book* from Natchez on April 6 saying that he had written a tale to Carey's specifications.[50] May 29 found him back in New York writing to the Harpers requesting a financial commitment from them. Requesting an advance on the sale of a manuscript was unusual during Ingraham's day, but a few best-selling authors did get advances, and Ingraham apparently felt his sales deserved them as well. Ingraham's letter is not his last on the subject, and it illustrates that Ingraham needed funds in a year that was, ostensibly, a prosperous one. He wrote:

> The merchant the planter the publisher and persons engaged in every branch of business are accustomed to anticipate the fruits of their labours & negotiations, through the facilities offered by the banks. Why then should not an author have the same privilege? He cannot live on air better than his neighbours. I have hired a house in N Brunswick [New Jersey] where I shall reside until I can build and remove to West Point. To enable me to furnish this house at once I want to anticipate the profits of my next work after the Quadroone. My brother B. J. Ingraham says if you will promise to pay me $750 towards it, within *30 days after you receive* The ms he will himself give me a check for the money. This you will see places you under no obligation whatever, while it will be doing me a great favor. It will also secure to you the right of publishing the novel when I have completed it.[51]

It appears that his appeal for money was in vain; *The Quadroone* was to be the last Harper-published novel, and there is no record that Ingraham built a house in West Point, New York. Other evidences exist that Ingraham anticipated his profits from his work, a practice that seems to have kept him continually in financial straits. He either could not manage his money or he had expenses not presently known.

The American Lounger, a collection of fourteen of Ingraham's short stories and essays, was dated from Philadelphia in June and dedicated to another Portland-born writer—Nathaniel Parker Willis. *Lounger* was the only Ingraham volume published by Philadelphia's Lea and Blanchard. The stories ranged from a legend of George Washington to one about the Hudson River Valley, from a tale about dueling in New Orleans to an historical essay on walking canes. At least three of the fourteen pieces had been previously published, and one other anticipates *The Quadroone* in several ways.

July 5 found the author in Philadelphia introducing the prolific Portland-born writer Mrs. Ann S. Stephens to his friends on the staff of *Godey's*.[52] Stephens had helped Ingraham earlier when she had edited *The Portland Sketch-Book* (1836); doubtless her connection with the *Ladies' Companion* had also furthered his career, and he was eager to aid her where he could. *The Southern Literary Messenger* reported in September that Ingraham intended "a voyage to England in the autumn,"[53] but the Professor either gave up his plans (how could he have afforded it?) or made a lightning trip, for he was in Buccleuch, New Jersey, on November 24.[54] From Buccleuch on December 10 he wrote another request for money to the Harpers. He noted that sickness in his family made his request necessary.[55] He continued: "I take this occasion of making you an offer of the American copy rights of my subsequent novels two a year for the next two years for $1500 each."[56] Again, his offer (and plea) was almost certainly declined, for the Harpers did not publish any Ingraham novels after *The Quadroone*.

Ingraham was lodged in the Sans Vinci Hotel in New York on January 31, 1840, from which he sent to the Harpers the first 150 pages of *The Quadroone* and a request for more money. The remainder of the novel was being copied by a secretary in preparation for the press since Ingraham's handwriting was only marginally legible.[57] The Professor's whereabouts for the rest of the year are unknown; perhaps it was during this time that Ingraham traveled to England.

The Quadroone; or, St. Michael's Day was finally published in 1841, though the first chapter of it had appeared in the *Democratic Review* in November, 1839, and an English edition had been printed in 1840.[58] Set in New Orleans in 1766 through 1769, the novel involves heroism and miscegenation; the latter was a daring subject for the times, but Ingraham clears his hero and heroine from any taint of Negro blood at the close of the tale in one of the most fantastically coincidental recognition scenes on record. The *Ladies' Companion* thought the novel was the best yet from the Professor's pen, but Poe's third review of an Ingraham novel was less enthusiastic.[59] Poe later wrote to Frederick W. Thomas on June 26:

It appears that Ingraham is in high dudgeon with me because I spoke ill of his "Quadroone." I am really sorry to hear it—but it is a matter that cannot be helped. As a man I like him much, and wherever I could do so, without dishonor to my own sense of truth, I have praised his writings. His "South-West," for example, I lauded highly. His "Quadroone" is, in my honest opinion, trash. If I must call it a good book to preserve the friendship of Prof. Ingraham—Prof. Ingraham may go to the devil.[60]

Poe never did call it a good book.

Poe made another comment about Ingraham in his "Autography" series for *Graham's Magazine* that November. In that series, the critic purported to characterize writers from their signatures. Under the Professor's signature Poe notes that

Mr. Ingraham, or Ingrahame (for he writes his name sometimes with, and sometimes without the *e*,) is one of our most *popular* novelists, if not one of our best. He appeals always to the taste of the ultraromanticists (as a matter, we believe, rather of pecuniary policy than of choice) and thus is obnoxious to the charge of a certain cut-and-thrust, blue-fire, melodramaticism. Still, he is capable of better things. His chirography is very unequal; at times sufficiently clear and flowing, at others, shockingly scratchy and uncouth. From it nothing whatever can be predicated, except an uneasy vacillation of temper and of purpose.[61]

Poe went quickly to the point. He knew Ingraham could write well, but he also knew that money could be made more easily by catering to public taste.

A new way of earning a dollar as well as more prestige occurred to Ingraham in June. He was in Washington, D.C., on June 15, and addressed a letter to Daniel Webster, the secretary of state.

I am now on my way to Europe on a literary tour and some of my friends having recently suggested to me that a connexion with a Foreign Embassy would place me in a position quite favorable to the object of that visit, I beg leave to enclose you one or two introductory letters & to ask your influence in my behalf. My acquaintance with the literature and customs of Spain, acquired chiefly by foreign travel incline me to give preference to that point. The advancement and elevation of American literature is the chief object of my visit abroad, and I shall feel both proud & happy, if, by your friendly approval, I can be placed in a position which will enable me both to serve my government and, at the same time, advance the literature of my country in a more desirable manner than, as a private individual, I otherwise could do.[62]

Ingraham did not receive an appointment; neither, it appears, did he go to Europe or Spain in 1841. He may have earlier as he says; several of his novels with Spanish and English settings do illustrate some acquaintance with the geography of the countries, but he could also have been stretching the truth. He apparently went abroad as a youth as mentioned earlier, but no records substantiate later travel.

Ingraham sold one more novel to the Harpers, but they did not publish it. The contract, dated from New York on October 8, says that "The Serf, or the Revolt of the Mexitili" was in Harper hands. No fee is mentioned. The two-volume novel was not published until 1845 and then by Henry L. Williams, one of the Williams brothers whose firms were to publish the bulk of Ingraham's work.

Casting around for another publisher as early as July, Ingraham wrote to George Roberts on the eighth. Roberts was the publisher of the *Boston Notion*, one of the so-called "mammoth weeklies" that gave the masses the cheap reading matter that they were beginning to devour. Few people would buy hardcover novels when they could buy a novel serially printed in a cheap weekly. Ingraham indicated that he had just completed "A Romance of Palanque" and offered it for serial publication in the *Notion*. There is no record that Roberts accepted the romance; neither is there an extant copy of the tale.

In August, still in New York, Ingraham wrote another letter about money; this time he owed money to W. H. Butterworth and could not pay. "It is with deep regret," wrote Ingraham, "and no trifling degree of mortification that I have been compelled, by unfavorable passing disappointments and vicissitudes, to withhold from you so long the amount due you." He goes on to note that his London publisher, Richard Bentley, owed him money, but he had not yet received it. "My disappointment in not receiving funds has rendered it necessary for me to send my family to the country to my father's and to take 'single lodging' "[63] in New York. The Professor was obviously in a precarious financial position. On August 24, he wrote an I.O.U. to Charles S. Rowell for twenty-five dollars which he promised to repay by September 1.

The results of the panic of 1837 had finally hit the Professor, and they had hit him hard. His lengthy, two-volume romances were not being published; and, although he sold over a dozen pieces to the periodicals in 1841, he obviously could not live on their earnings. Something had to be done. English novels were selling more cheaply than native American works because, in the absence of a copyright law, American publishers could pirate and publish English works at little expense. The situation was noted by William Gilmore Simms in a letter to John Henry Hammond on August 16. Even "Ingraham," wrote Simms, "could scarcely at this time get a novel published at all—certainly he could hope to get nothing for it. The publishers are very costive—the sales are terribly diminished within the last few years. . . . In this country an Edition now instead of 4 or 5,000 copies, is scarce 2,000."[64] This comment is interesting because it notes Simms' knowledge of Ingraham, but it also shows that Simms underrated the Professor, for Ingraham was to prove that sales were possible, though not in the two-volume hardbound format.

III A Change of Direction

Ingraham had to publish to eat and to get out of debt. He had not found a vocation so consistently satisfying as authorship, and he did not plan to give it up. He thus decided to try the *Boston Notion* again. Its editors accepted *The Dancing Feather*, another pirate tale, and the novel began to appear serially in the paper on November 27, 1841. *The Dancing Feather*'s appearance marked the beginning of a new phase in the Professor's career. The days of the long, leisurely novels were seemingly over. He soon began to manufacture quickly written paperbound novels that usually ranged in length from thirty to one hundred finely printed double-columned pages. That he "ventured to make his living from his books during depression years . . . [indicated] his confidence in his ability to turn out salable fiction fast."[65]

Ingraham may have moved to Boston in 1842 to be near his publishers, but the year saw only the publication of *The Dancing Feather* and one other novel in book form. Then a second chance for government service appeared when he received an appointment to proceed to the Isthmus of Panama "to inquire into the ability of the people . . . to maintain their independence"[66] after a revolution. But another revolution erupted before Ingraham could leave, and Daniel Webster, the secretary of state, wrote the Professor on February 11 to inform him that "the agency which was to have been conferred upon Mr. Ingraham in relation to the States of Panama and Veragua is rendered unnecessary." The disappointed Ingraham applied for no more foreign service appointments.

At least it was a successful year in periodical contributions (a minimum of eighteen pieces), but these publications were not enough to stave off bankruptcy for the author, who was compelled to take the debtor's oath "from inability to meet a debt for which I was security." What that debt was is not known. Ingraham was at the lowest financial ebb of his career, but his spirit remained unbroken. He wrote that "I hope, however, yet to rise superior to my reverses and pay those friends to whom I am indebted."[67]

George Roberts' publication of *The Dancing Feather* sold twenty thousand copies even after it was published in the *Notion*,[68] but Ingraham must not have received any money from the sale or he surely would not have gone bankrupt. He switched publishers, but it was not until 1843 that he found another book firm with which he could feel comfortable. These publishers were the Bostonians Edward P. and Henry L. Williams, who published under several separate imprints—all from their single Congress Street address. These firms issued most of Ingraham's works from 1843 until 1847, and his output during that time was so prodigious that one critic estimated the Professor single-handedly "accounted for nearly 10 per cent of the fiction titles published during the 'forties."[69] Unfortunately, the records of the Williams' publishing concerns are no longer extant; they were probably burned in the "fire of 1872 which engulfed most of Congress Street and ravaged a number of publishing houses."[70] Those records could have told us much about Ingraham's career at its most prolific, if not its most critically successful, period.

In 1843, Ingraham published at least eight books[71] in addition to his periodical output. Even this number was not enough to avoid the press of debt. He wrote his lawyers, the New York firm of Ketchum and Fessenden, on November 7, telling them that Mrs. Ingraham had had a long and "unusually expensive" illness, that he was "wholly dependent" on his pen, and that he would do what he could "towards the payment of . . . [his] debt" but that he could promise nothing.[72] Prosperity still eluded the Professor's grasp.

Ingraham realized that he had to turn out relatively short pieces of fiction in order to get them printed, but he did not give up the two-volume format without a fight. One of his favorite ways to evade cutting down his stories was to leave them unfinished and promise his readers that sequels were on the way. He had first used this expedient with *The Dancing Feather*. The 1843 sequel was *Morris Graeme: or, the Cruise of the Sea-Slipper*. In an introduction to *Graeme*, Ingraham explained that he had originally intended *The Dancing Feather* to reach the fifty-chapter length usually employed by two-volume novels, but his editor, after Ingraham had produced six chapters, requested that the tale be limited to ten. Thus, the author was forced to cut his projections, and that is why a few apparent errors crept into the end of *Feather* and why the novel was not ended to everyone's satisfaction. Ingraham promised that the sequel would clear up all the loose ends of the earlier story. For the next few years he protested against having to shorten his novels until, finally, in 1845, he was permitted a legitimate two-volume creation and another one the next year.

Ingraham rebelled against the prevailing strictures of the public in another way. The "predominantly female fiction-reading public"[73] generally expected a happy ending or a moral or both, but Ingraham did not always oblige them. In *Frank Rivers* [1843], a man uses a hatchet to cleave the skull of a woman that he seduced; then he escapes. In *Arnold* (1844), Benedict Arnold escapes punishment for his treachery. A hunchback kills the title character in *Herman De Ruyter* (1844) and escapes. There are several other instances in which seducers of young women get away with their wicked deeds, but these examples are representative.

Reviewers generally ignored Ingraham's paperback novels. Presumably he was no longer considered a serious author, but another reason might be that he was publishing too rapidly for the reviewers to keep up. The Professor used endless plot variations, but he stayed close to tales of pirates (and other sea adventures) and moralistic stories that compared and contrasted the joys of country life with the evils and debaucheries of big cities like Boston or New York. Since there is an undeniable sameness about many of these tales, the reviewers may be at least partially forgiven for their silence.

However one regards the tales of these years, he must remember that they sold. They would not have been printed otherwise. Ingraham published nineteen novels and about fifteen pieces in various periodicals in 1844. *The Dancing Feather* was dramatized and presented in Philadelphia that year;[74] again, no copy survives. The year is also notable in that the first and only widely circulated portrait of Ingraham appeared facing the title page of *Santa Claus*. The novel is worthless, but the picture tells volumes. The seated author has a noble bearing and is expensively dressed; he wears a full-length coat with vest and cravat. A dark, carefully sculptured beard outlines his profiled face. Dark, dashing, highly romantic—he must have looked exactly as his readers pictured him.

The peak of Ingraham's book production was reached in 1845 when he published twenty-five novels. The Portland *Eastern Argus* reported on March 22 that the Professor received fifty dollars apiece for his novels "and the everlasting gratitude of his publishers."[75] The article continued by noting that Ingraham was currently living in a small village in Maine; a later story would identify that village as Bath.

It is almost inconceivable that an author who published as much as Ingraham should still have financial problems, but he did. From Boston, on April 3, 1846, he wrote to J. B. Staples requesting an extension on a loan. Ingraham writes:

To pay you from my regular monthly receipts would hardly give you ten dollars a month, for I have scarcely that over my expenses. My income just keeps me along without debt, of which I have the greatest horror, for I have suffered a very great deal thereby. I have not asked a pecuniary favor of any body for three years and a half nearly. I have made just enough to get along and pay some small debts. . . . I have had a very sick family, for the most part of this winter Mrs Ingraham & both of my children [Prentiss (1843-1904) and Josephine Scott?] have been under the physician's hands, and they are not now well enough for me to leave them.[76]

If Ingraham had not borrowed any money for three and a half years, it is possible that his unspecified debt to Staples dates from his 1842 bankruptcy and that he was trying to pay off his old debts.

Three days later, on April 6, Ingraham visited Henry Wadsworth Longfellow who later wrote in his journal: "In the afternoon, Ingraham the novelist called. A young, dark man, with soft voice. He says he has written eighty novels, and of these twenty during the last year; till it has grown to be merely mechanical with him. These novels are published in the newspapers. They pay him something more than three thousand dollars a year."[77] If Ingraham's novels were still being first published in newspapers, they have not yet been located, and it is possible that they will never be located, since many of the popular literary newspapers of the day are lost. The other notable facet of Longfellow's entry is the reference to Ingraham's income: "No other novelist North or South was consistently earning as much as that in the 1840's."[78] And yet it was not enough.

CHAPTER 2

The Minister

I *Vocation Changed*

INGRAHAM must have realized that he could not keep on producing books in quantity forever. His production was down to sixteen titles in 1846 and dropped to ten in 1847; he was probably simply exhausted from the strain of writing and trying to hatch new plots so quickly. In 1847, he seriously contemplated the momentous change he had thought about as early as 1830 — the idea of entering the ministry. He would be giving up a great deal to become a minister because he would lose much of his fame as a writer by failing to publish one or two new works a year. He seemed unlikely to improve his financial condition: ministers were certainly not well paid, and Ingraham would have to study several years before he could be ordained and given a church. It would take genuine courage to leave a career, uncertain as it was, to begin another career even more full of uncertainties. But Ingraham had the courage and genuine faith in God's providence.

A careful reader of Ingraham's novels will not be too surprised that the writer would choose the ministry. Throughout many of his novels runs the idea that God is behind the wonders of nature, that God would protect the poor, the homeless, the sick. When a major Ingraham character would reach the deepest level of despair, poverty, and want, he would often resign himself to God's care, and the individual's faith was never misplaced. Ingraham may have even written himself into the ministry through the faith of some of his characters, but a more conservative view is that his brother, John Phillip Thurston Ingraham, influenced him to study theology.[1] J. P. T. Ingraham was already a minister of the Protestant Episcopal Church, and it was in this faith that J. H. Ingraham was confirmed in 1847.[2]

Ingraham was in Natchez in March, 1847, to attend the term examinations at Jefferson College.[3] He probably rested for a while at Rose Cottage before he moved to Nashville, Tennessee, in September to live and study theology in preparation for taking orders in the church.[4] His preparation would take at least three years.[5]

To meet the problem of supporting himself and his family while in Nashville, Ingraham turned again to teaching and became principal of the Vine Street Female Academy or Christ Church School.[6] It appears that he began the school for young ladies in the basement room of Christ Church almost immediately upon his arrival in Nashville. It moved to new quarters on Vine Street on April 11, 1849.[7] He charged the pupils twenty-five dollars each for a session of five months and taught them French, Spanish, drawing, bookkeeping, and Latin;[8] but he soon discovered that many of his students could not read, possibly because Nashville had no public schools at that time. Some of the girls, as young as ten, were boarded in Ingraham's home.[9]

Tennessee had money for a free school system. The schools, known as "pauper schools," were created by an 1815 act and an 1823 law which levied taxes on a number of items to provide funds to educate the poor and the children orphaned by the War of 1812. Families of means did not want their children to go to pauper schools, and they were not interested in being taxed for schools their children did not attend.[10] Ingraham, who had seen the effect of public schools in the North as well as in Natchez, began a battle to educate the people to the advantages of a free public school system supported by property taxes.

Toward this end he used his pen again to produce a *Report Upon a Proposed System of Public Education, for the City of Nashville, Respectfully Addressed to the Citizens.* He delivered his address to a meeting of the town's citizens on June 7, 1848. The next day Mayor Allison and the aldermen of the city requested Ingraham to publish the address so that all in the city might become familiar with its arguments.[11]

Its arguments were persuasive. Ingraham pointed out that free public schools would lower the schooling costs of those who owned property by doing away with the numerous expensive private schools. He documented with many facts and figures that if people were more educated, they might stay out of jail—a strong argument, since the state was then spending more on

The Minister

prisoners than on schools. In an appendix to the *Report*, he printed the rules under which the free public schools of Natchez operated.

Spurred on by the interest shown by city officials, Ingraham addressed a June 27 letter to Horace Mann, one of the most eminent educators of the day. He sent Mann a copy of his *Report* and told him that

> My object in writing is to desire you to take the trouble of transmitting to me as early as possible, such documents touching the Public School system as will be best adapted to *inform* the minds of a committee of gentlemen, who otherwise sufficiently intelligent, have not given to this subject any attention whatsoever.
> In bringing the subject of Public schools before the people here and urging it upon their adoption, I have done all that is in my power to do, as all my time is occupied in preparing for orders, and in teaching a school of Thirty young ladies, in the unoccupied hours of which duties I gave myself to drawing up my Report. The mayor & City Council & all the influential men in the city have warmly taken up the subject and say they must carry the school at the municipal Elections in September, which will turn upon this question alone—"school or no school."[12]

To this plea for assistance, Ingraham added his proposals for school buildings and their possible enrollment ("two buildings central in each half of the city, capable of containing 700 or 800 scholars") as well as the information that some donors were willing to contribute to the cause if Mann could help with more information. On October 5, 1848, the *Nashville Whig* reported that 668 people voted for state-financed public schools for all while 137 voted against them.[13]

Mann did not answer Ingraham's letter, but Ingraham did not give up so easily and wrote the educator again on November 1 and added even more details about his proposals.

> I am very much aware that you must be very troubled by applications touching information upon your admirable common school system which has made Massachusetts so eminently superior in intelligence and mental power, to other states. If I could obtain what I seek this side of you I would not encroach upon your time. . . .
> This city contains twenty one thousand inhabitants, is well-built, with a population free from poor immigrants its situation being out of the usual track of emigration. There are but very few poor (as you may judge when I say we have no poor-house in the city). The lower class

are principally mechanics. The city is two miles long and half a mile wide—a centre with two equal wings. . . .The plan I have thought of is this: If you will look at the [enclosed] diagram you will see an addendum marked [s]. This is a five acre lot lately presented to the city by a deceased gentleman for the public schools, with a wish that the buildings should be erected upon it. It is situated just on the verge of the centre of the city, as about equidistant from the wings. It is not more than twenty-five minutes walk from the extremities of the city. I have therefore thought that a central High School might be erected here capable of containing fourteen hundred scholars, and that a primary school with five hundred seats in each [less than his first proposal], might be placed in each wing of the city where I have placed a cross X. This primary school to be central for smaller children and include such as are too young to walk so far as [s] and comprise a department as high as nine years at which age they enter the lowest department at [s].

I stand almost alone, sir, in this public school question, and have no one to advise with. . . . I have Mr. [Augustus] Barnard's book which is of great value, and has been of service to me.

. . . Your name here, sir, will be sufficient alone to ensure the unanimous adoption of any system for the city you may suggest.[14]

It appears that Mann did not answer Ingraham's second appeal for help either, and public schools supported by property taxes in Nashville (and in Tennessee) did not become a reality until Governor Andrew Johnson got the necessary law passed in 1854, several years after Ingraham had left Nashville. Johnson was as much of a crusader as Ingraham because the governor, due to the lack of public schools, reached manhood "without [the] ability to do more than barely read."[15] Johnson was also aware of the value of an education and what it could mean to people.

Ingraham had discovered another cause while in Nashville, one he connected closely with the need for public education. Very shortly after his arrival, he became interested in the state penitentiary. He visited the prison and learned that the prisoners were relatively humanely treated but discovered that the convicts had no chaplain and were confined to their cells on Sundays. Ingraham, after much argument with Warden McIntosh, was given permission to talk with, and read the Bible to, the men on Sundays. Thus, the first congregation that Ingraham addressed, in an unofficial capacity, was composed of the prisoners of the Tennessee State Penitentiary. He kept the prisoners' attention and earned their respect. Although paid nothing for his work, he visited the prison every Sunday for three years.[16] What this unpaid candidate for religious orders accomplished is as totally admirable as it is totally forgotten.

Ingraham discovered that "out of two hundred men within the penitentiary, one hundred and twenty could not both read and write" and was confirmed in his belief that crime often resulted from lack of education. Single-handedly he taught about thirty men to read[17] and presented a class of thirty men to his bishop for confirmation. He drew up a petition and presented it to the state legislature requesting that a chaplain be appointed for the prisoners. The governor signed the bill and offered Ingraham the job, but because Ingraham was not yet ordained, he could not accept; the prison records do not even mention Ingraham's role in proposing this legislation.[18]

Bishop J. H. Otey, however, did commend Ingraham's work in his 1850 annual report to the Diocese of Tennessee.

I attended at the Penitentiary [on May 12] for the purpose of administering confirmation to a number of the convicts, who had been instructed and prepared for this rite chiefly, by the labors of Mr. Jos. H. Ingraham, one of our candidates for orders. Mr. Ingraham has been laboring for two years with great diligence and zeal to improve the religious character of these unhappy and unfortunate men. He undertook this work with my consent and approbation and under the sanction of the authority of the State. His efforts deserve and will, I doubt not, receive the hearty commendation of every true follower of Christ and every lover of his kind, while the approbation of his own conscience, next to the favor of God, will be his richest reward.[19]

The *Nashville Daily Gazette* for October 30, 1849, also noted Ingraham's contribution to the prison and stated that "Prof. I. deserves much credit for his benevolent efforts at the prison, laboring as he did, without pay or compensation."[20] The *Gazette* also reported that Ingraham had recommended a chapel and a hospital for the prison and that both could be constructed under one roof.

The Reverend J. P. T. Ingraham was, at this time, assistant rector of Christ Church in Nashville and occasionally helped his brother by baptizing inmates of the prison. J. H. Ingraham, in his own annual report for 1850, thanked the Reverend Ingraham for his help and noted that "The gospel seems to find its true and proper field where men are most lost!"[21] The candidate had entered his new vocation with a wholly admirable devotion and dedication.

Still another project began to take shape in 1850. This project, a literary one, took the form of a series of letters that began publication in August in *The Evergreen, A Repository of Religious, Literary and Entertaining Knowledge, for the Christian Family.* The first of thirty-four installments (containing thirty-nine letters) bore the title "Letters from Adina, Daughter of Manasseh, The Rich Jew of Alexandria, to Her Father. Written from Jerusalem in the Days of Pontius Pilate; Translated from the Alexandrian MSS. in the *Biblioteque Antique* of Cairo, in Egypt." Ingraham was going back to novel writing, but his subject had changed from the secular to the biblical. "Adina" was the first of three major biblical romances he was to write, but it is the only one known to have been begun in Nashville. In 1855, the epistolary tale was renamed *The Prince of the House of David* and published by the obscure New York firm of Pudney & Russell. The *Evergreen* had a limited circulation since it was primarily an Episcopal periodical, but the same was not true of the novel. *Prince* is listed by one writer as an "over-all" bestseller in the years before the Civil War.[22] A sale of 225,000 copies was required to make this list, but no one really knows how many copies the novel has sold. Another critic claims it had sold between four and five million copies by 1931.[23] The novel continued to sell well, and remained in print into the 1970s, although the last edition, published by Collins in London, is considerably abridged.

II Back to Mississippi

Ingraham left Nashville on or before January 1, 1851,[24] and returned to Mississippi for his first official assignment. He was ordained a deacon by Mississippi Bishop William Mercer Green on March 9, 1851,[25] and appointed to the missionary post of Aberdeen. When he arrived there on April 2, 1851,[26] he had charge of St. John's Church. Ingraham was also responsible for Grace Church in Okolona and St. Paul's Church in Columbus. The first Sunday in every month found him at Okolona; the

The Minister

second and fourth Sundays were spent in Aberdeen, and on the third Sunday he journeyed to Columbus.[27]

Ingraham's arrival in Aberdeen marked the beginning of the continuous existence of St. John's and the start of a program to build a new church.[28] After nine months, he reported:

"It is with gratitude to God that I am able to report this parish in a highly prosperous condition, and presenting a most encouraging field for the Church. Indeed, the whole of the rich valley of the Tombigbee, which has direct commerce in the cotton season with Mobile, is a worthy field for missionary labour. The population is of the best class— is wealthy, is increasing, and without prejudices. The Church is received with kindness and confidence. When your missionary entered upon this field of labour in March, there were but eight communicants known to be here, and no Church, though by the instrumentality of pious women several hundred dollars had been raised. Now there are eighteen communicants, many candidates for confirmation, a Gothic Church 70 by 36 feet, which will cost $3,000, to be built of brick, in progress, to be completed by Christmas, and an increasing congregation. Two hundred dollars are also subscribed towards an organ; and our chancel furniture is all to be presented to us by ladies in New-Orleans.

"Four hours' ride from here, at the prairie village of Okelona [sic], finding several Church people providentially settled near one another, I organized a parish, under the style of Grace Church. . . . We at once raised one thousand dollars, and a piece of land being presented to us, we contracted with an architect to put up a neat Gothic Church with a spire, the whole to be completed also by Christmas day. The money for this Church, and $2,300 for the one here, is all paid in, as we have a holy horror of going into debt."[29]

Ingraham laid the cornerstone of St. John's on October 16 and was in Pontotoc organizing a new parish—Trinity Church—on November 26. In Okolona, on December 18, he laid the cornerstone of Grace Church.[30]

Ingraham was ordained to the priesthood in St. Andrew's Church of Jackson, Mississippi, on February 8, 1852, by Bishop Green. When he was in Natchez several days later, the *Mississippi Free Trader* commented that

A few days since we saw the dark and intellectual features of the author of "Lafitte the Pirate of the Gulf," and various other romantic legends and narratives, in our streets. We noticed a somewhat unusual longitude of countenance and the white cravat, very much at variance with the former jaunty, dashing, imposing, mustachioed, half-bandit air of the same gentleman years since on the paves of Philadelphia and New York, with silver-mounted pistol and jeweled attaghan in belt.[31]

The cause for this change, the article goes on, was Ingraham's ordination to the priesthood.

The new minister was soon back in Aberdeen delivering the first of a series of extremely well-received lectures on astronomy at the Aberdeen Female College.[32] He now had more time to work and stay in Aberdeen because he had been able to resign his Columbus charge to a new minister in December; the church he had founded in Pontotoc had another minister in January, and an additional minister had been assigned to Okolona by April.[33] He was now able to preach at 10:30 A.M. and 3:30 P.M. every Sunday in Aberdeen.[34]

Besides having time for lectures, Ingraham had more time for one of his favorite topics—public education supported by property taxes. In late March he and several others appeared before an audience "in reference to a permanent High School or College." The Aberdeen *Monroe Democrat* for March 24 announced that, on the occasion of these addresses, the brass band would play, and, "it is hoped, . . . contribute to the interest of the occasion."[35] Obviously the Aberdeen citizens needed more enticement than the ones at Nashville, although the end result of the meeting was the same—no free public schools.

Ingraham went back to focusing his labors on his still incomplete church. Despairing of getting a local architect, he designed and helped in the construction of the church himself. He later reported that he built the church "with two young men and eight colored mechanics. The style is Elizabethan. The body or nave is 70 by 37; the tower 14 feet square and 70 feet in height, terminating in parapet and four turrets. Seven flat Norman arches span the ceiling with corbels pending in the centres. There is a triple-lancet window above the chancel, and a vestry-room with embrasured parapet, turrets and buttresses in keeping with the main building."[36] Ingraham also helped build the new Gothic-style church at Okolona. These projects indicate how diversified Ingraham's talents and activities were.

The Minister

Ingraham was also self-sacrificing. A minister in his era was usually paid from the rent of the pews in his church. Because he did not want to see his congregation in debt, he "resigned all the rents of the pews, $1,150, . . . to pay off the last bill against the church." Since he contributed his salary to the church, he had "to teach all day as professor in the Methodist Female Institute . . . to enable . . . [himself] to find bread for . . . [his] butter."[37] In another year, he believed, the bills would be paid and he could receive his salary as well as devote more time to his ecclesiastical duties.

St. John's was finally finished in April, 1853. Each of the sixty-eight pews rented for twenty-five dollars, and the congregation could bid on choice locations if they wished.[38] Ingraham kept teaching, however, until August, 1853. In that month he interfered in some way with the punishment of a servant at the Institute and was dismissed. Owing, no doubt, at least partly to his dismissal, Ingraham resigned his rectorship of St. John's and was back in Natchez in September.[39]

He was not to be idle long however, for in November, 1853, he accepted a call to another St. John's Church, this one located in Mobile, Alabama. He took up his duties on December 18 and was to be paid a salary of fifteen hundred dollars a year.[40] In this same month, his serialization of the "Letters from Adina" was finished. St. John's Church had just been completed, so the Reverend Ingraham again became the first minister of a new church. The church was completely paid for when Ingraham arrived, and he noted with satisfaction that his church owed no man anything but love.[41]

Ingraham's salary was guaranteed by the members of the Vestry, for since St. John's Mobile was deeded to the parish as a free church, there was no rent charged on the pews—a bold and relatively new idea in 1853. Ingraham's salary was to come from the weekly offerings, and, if the offerings did not total fifteen hundred dollars, the vestrymen would make up this deficit.[42] Ingraham, however, still must have had a hard time making financial ends meet because he had turned to teaching again.[43] He also kept up his efforts with his pen. Some of his parishioners must have commented unfavorably upon his earlier, occasionally gory, adventure novels because when *Lafitte* was reprinted in 1853 by DeWitt and Davenport, Ingraham was definitely upset. That republication, along with the reprinting of several other of his novels, caused Ingraham to address a letter to the editor of the *Churchman,* a letter that was published in several newspapers.

> Rev. and Dear Sir [wrote Ingraham]:—The recent *re-issue* of several works of fiction and tales under my name, compels me to publish the present card, *disclaiming* all interest in, or permission for, such republications. . . . Since 1846 I have not published anything under my own name. . . . As I never retained copy-rights of my earlier books, and as my magazine and newspaper tales were uncopyrighted, I, of course, have *no control* whatsoever over these works. . . . My surprise and mortification therefore, now that I am devoted wholly to the duties of a minister of the Gospel, I cannot adequately express.[44]

The letter can be taken at face value—he was upset about his early novels being reprinted—but he was probably even more upset that he was not collecting royalties from them.

A situation involving Ingraham's religious beliefs and his friend Bishop Green of Mississippi arose in 1854 when the Reverend Richard Abbey attacked Episcopal doctrines and assailed Green in a series of published statements. Ingraham took up his pen in defense of both the doctrines and Green. *Pamphlets for the People. In Illustration of the Claims of the Church and Methodism,* a thirteen-essay attack aimed at the offending minister, was published anonymously in 1854. Keeping on his cloak of anonymity, Ingraham published some letters in the *Philadelphia Saturday Courier* under the name of Miss Kate Conyngham.[45] These letters praised and defended Southern life in a much more extravagant vein than *The South-West* had.

Another set of letters, the "Letters from Adina," finished in 1853, were published in 1855 as *The Prince of the House of David.* Appearing in the same year as Walt Whitman's *Leaves of Grass, Prince* was a trailblazer of a different sort. It was the "first Biblical novel to enjoy an enormous and continuing success."[46] Ingraham's epistolary romance contains nothing new in technique or writing ability; he had hit, however, on the most popular fusion of fact and fiction he would ever accomplish, even though two more novels based on the Bible were yet to come.

No one knows the financial arrangements Ingraham made with his publisher, but they could not have been favorable to him. He must have sold his right to *Prince* for a one-time fee, for he was in financial straits again in less than a year after the novel's publication. His conscience would not allow him to continue to depend on the vestrymen of St. John's to supplement his salary, and he released them from their pledge in December, 1855. The offertory alone, however, was not sufficient to pay his salary, so, on July 6, 1856, he informed his parishioners that he would have to relinquish his rectorship because the offertory was less than expected. His sense of duty would not let him resign until October since cholera and yellow fever were frequent visitors to deep South summers, and a replacement minister would be hard to find.[47] Ingraham was as considerate as he was evidently virtually penniless. Some believe Ingraham spent the money earned from *Prince* (and from his other religious novels) to buy up and destroy the copyrights of his earlier romances[48] since he felt embarrassed by them after becoming a minister, but specific data is lacking to prove such an assertion.

Ingraham did resign but did not preach his farewell sermon until January 11, 1857. He had been a faithful rector. "No word of criticism or dissatisfaction can be found regarding . . . [his] discharge of his parochial ministry."[49] From Mobile, he moved to Baltimore, Maryland,[50] for a few months where he could again be closer to the major publishing centers.

Ingraham reestablished contact with Harper & Brothers through Fletcher Harper and, on March 17, from Baltimore, wrote Harper that anything of his accepted for publication was to be published anonymously.[51] By March 23, Ingraham had mailed to the Harpers a series of articles entitled "The Romance of Astronomy."[52] These articles were presumably based on the lectures Ingraham delivered in Aberdeen in 1852, but they were never printed. *Harper's New Monthly Magazine* did eventually print five brief tales by Ingraham, but they mark no advance in any area over his previous work.

By May 12, Ingraham had accepted a call to St. Andrew's Church in Riverside, Tennessee. Here he was also to be the head of Riverside Hall, "an institution for young ladies," which was connected with St. Andrew's Church. Riverside, near modern-day Vonore, Tennessee, was "thirty miles from Knoxville . . . [and was] situated upon the [Little] Tennessee river."[53] The site was near the present restoration of Fort Loudon,[54] though the traces of the church are now erased.

Ingraham's service at St. Andrew's was brief through no fault of his own. The church, another new one, had been built by people more infused with the love of the cross as a symbol than with the teachings of Episcopal doctrine. The builders of St. Andrew's seemed to have leaned toward "a system known as *symbolism,* and which is commonly associated in the public mind with some of the most palpable errors and gross corruptions in the teaching of Romanism."[55] When Tennessee Bishop Otey arrived to consecrate the church on August 8, he was displeased. He "beheld a cross on every gate, three crosses on the roof, and one on the belfry. On entering the Church, he found the font at the south door of the Church; and on the altar and super-altar, a large movable cross, two vases for flowers, two very long candlesticks, and five other crosses with multiform deities upon them."[56] This multitude of crosses not only struck the good bishop as signs of Romanism but also as "a lamentable proof of the absence of an instructed faith, an enlightened conscience, and a sound mind. . . . I, therefore, orderly, calmly and deliberately, without violence or harshness of word or manner, directed the minister in charge to take the candlesticks and moveable cross into the vestry-room." The bishop would not consecrate the church that day but did the next after some assurances that the symbols would be removed.[57]

But some problems must still have remained, for Ingraham had resigned his charge by February, 1858. The *Natchez Weekly Courier* explained that "A question growing out of the validity of the consecration of the church, and the impossibility of obtaining a satisfactory title and deeds of donation to the buildings . . . has rendered it necessary for the Rector to send in his resignation." Ingraham moved to Knoxville for a short while but was back in Natchez by June at least.[58] St. Andrew's had a few more ministers, but the church was closed during the Civil War and never reopened.[59]

In Natchez, Ingraham was temporarily in charge of Trinity Church while the Reverend Perry, the assigned rector, was out of town.[60] Ingraham's month at Trinity Church produced one of his two extant sermons. (The other dates from 1852 and Aberdeen, Mississippi.) The untitled sermon is on the divinity of the Holy Ghost and was printed in both the *Natchez Daily Courier* and the *Natchez Weekly Courier.*[61] His address produced

The Minister

a most laudatory comment by an unnamed parishioner, one of the few comments we have on Ingraham's preaching:

> Mr. Ingraham very forcibly reminds me of the characteristics peculiar to the Norse-giants; he has the same astonishing vigor, and the same lofty, difficulty-defying nature. He has stood forth as an original prophet of modern times, and he resembles the last of the ancient prophets in this—that his words have often been like a "voice in the wilderness." With a glance which has penetrated deep into the world of history and spirit; with a heart glowing with Christian inspiration; with a voice, which now resembles the power of mighty thunderings, and now the soft cadence of rippling streams, he has stood forward, preaching return to the living faith, a new birth into the spirit of the ancient times, as the only salvation from spiritual, intellectual and political perdition. . . . Nature has indeed endowed him with that miraculous power which is called genius, the power of a deeper, clearer, more rapid intention, of feeling more warmly and more noble, than the multitude.[62]

The writer may have been carried away a bit with his own rhetoric, but the comment remains valuable as a testimony to the regard in which Ingraham was held.

When the Reverend Perry returned to Trinity Church, Ingraham was freed for another assignment which was not long in coming. He was called to Christ Church in Holly Springs, Mississippi, on July 1, 1858, and arrived there on September 13, again to take charge of a new church.[63] His brief service at Trinity Church in Natchez was the only work he did in an established church. He preached his first sermon in Holly Springs on September 19; the church was consecrated by Bishop Green on October 7.[64] Besides being rector of Christ Church, Ingraham also had charge of St. Thomas Hall, a school for boys.[65] He was soon at work with his usual enthusiasm.

Ingraham was also busy with his second biblical novel; *The Pillar of Fire; or, Israel in Bondage,* dated from Holly Springs on January 1, 1859, is the tale of the Egyptian bondage of the Hebrews and of Moses, who arose to deliver them from their captors. Like *The Prince of the House of David*, it is an epistolary novel and contains letters supposedly composed by three different individuals. Ingraham would have been most flattered to see, almost a hundred years later, that Cecil B. DeMille used his volume as source material for the film director's 1956 production of *The Ten Commandments.*

Ingraham was honored on July 13, 1859, by the University of Mississippi.[66] The university recognized his contribution to the church and the literary world as it awarded him the LL.D. degree. Ingraham's personal popularity had possibly never been higher.

He found time, on November 8, 1859, to write a lengthy note to Anne M. Hall in England, who had written a complimentary letter about his *Prince of the House of David.* What Ingraham most appreciated, it seems, was that Mrs. Hall had not characterized his novel as a religious one.

God forbid [he wrote] that I should for a moment harbour a thought so wicked & impious as to make my crucified & beloved Lord and Saviour the central figure of a fiction. The work was perceived, every line of it with "reverence & godly fear." I wrote it as a commentary on the gospels of the life & acts & words of Jesus. . . . I know the book has been an instrument of good; of sending hundreds to the pages of their neglected Bible. I have numerous letters of gratitude from perfect strangers who write to me that the perusal of that Book has brought them to the knowledge of Jesus and to embrace Christianity.[67]

Ingraham also told Mrs. Hall that *Prince* had gone into two German translations and that he hoped he would soon be coming through London on his way to Germany; he probably did not make the trip, for no evidence exists that he left Holly Springs for any great length of time.

The next year brought Ingraham's *The Sunny South* and his third religious novel. *The Sunny South* is a collection of letters about life in the South written, supposedly, by a young Northern governess from 1853 to 1856. Some of the letters had previously appeared in the Philadelphia *Saturday Courier* in 1853 and 1854.[68] Ingraham's third and final biblical novel is dated from Holly Springs on January 26, 1860. *The Throne of David* concerns the reigns of Saul and David and is the third volume of the author's trilogy on the Hebrews. In chronological order, *The Pillar of Fire* is the first chapter in the history of the Hebrews; *The Throne of David* is the second; and *The Prince of the House of David* completes the trilogy. One reviewer of the 603-page *Throne* succinctly noted that "After reading it, one can turn back to the concise statements of the Bible with new appreciation."[69]

The Minister 47

Ingraham had begun his career writing two-volume works, and it seems he could not be comfortable unless he had that much space in which to maneuver.

Ingraham called on his friend Benjamin L. C. Wailes in early summer with a proposal to rent Wailes' Washington, Mississippi, home. He told Wailes he was thinking of giving up full-time ministerial duties and devoting most of his time to "preaching through Books."[70] But Ingraham did not retire as he planned.

Ingraham visited New York in November to find a publisher for his next novel.[71] He approached George Carleton with a request for a three thousand-dollar advance on *St. Paul the Roman Citizen.* Carleton declined the proposition when he learned Ingraham had not yet written the work.[72] It is true that Ingraham had not completed the work, but he had already begun it: ten parts of it had been printed in 1856 under the title "Elfrida, the Druid's Daughter; or, The Cross Planted in Britain. A Tale of the First Century."[73] The tale began well, but its conclusion was too quickly reached; Ingraham had much room for expansion, but it is surprising that Carleton would refuse such a popular author. Ingraham returned to Holly Springs and his parish duties on December 5. Aunt Rosie (Mrs. S. L. Falconer), one of his parishioners, said that Ingraham was "Looking improved in health and spirits" despite being rejected by Carleton and that the town was pleased to have him back.[74]

Ingraham's son Prentiss later retold the events of that fateful December.

"The country was on the verge of a civil war and lawlessness had begun to prevail. . . . Ingraham . . . as a matter of precaution left a revolver at a gunsmith's to be repaired; the key to the vestry-room of his church had also been left there to be mended; and when he called for it, the revolver was wrapped up and handed to him. Driving to the church to try the key, he opened the door, and as he did so, some papers were blown to the floor; as he stooped to gather them up, the package containing the revolver slipped from his grasp,—the weapon had been loaded by the gunsmith who failed to mention the fact,—and as the package struck the floor, a chamber exploded, the bullet penetrating the leg above the knee, and ranging upward into the body. Not realizing that he had been seriously injured, Doctor Ingraham picked up the revolver, left the church and hurried to his carriage. Then the dangerous nature of the wound became evident; for nine days he lingered in intense agony, and died as he had hoped to die, conscious to the last, and with his family and friends around him."[75]

Ingraham died on December 18.[76] Bishop Green of Mississippi and Bishop Otey of Tennessee came to officiate at the funeral, and ministers of different denominations were his pallbearers. Aunt Rosie described the funeral in a fashion that would have pleased the romantic rector:

The crowd at Church was immense; business houses were closed and business suspended for the time; numbers not being able to enter the Church. As the long procession left the Church and wound its way along to the final home of all living, the sun was just sinking below the horizon, and its lingering rays lighted up the heavens with a glowing radiant light—the floating clouds were burnished with golden circles; the distant storm cloud muttered and mourned as if in sympathy with mortality; and when the procession reached the cemetery, and the coffin was laid above the cold open grave, the very heavens seemed to grow solemn and the pattering rain drops, as they fell upon the coffin, and the sighing winds seemed to chant a solemn requiem for the departed. At the head of the grave stood two Bishops; with uncovered heads, and the solemn words of the burial service broke the awful stillness, every head was uncovered and every heart full. The dear body was then laid away to sleep in its narrow bed until the final resurrection.[77]

Mary Brookes Ingraham survived her husband only a year;[78] nothing is known of the rest of Ingraham's family except of his son Prentiss, who also became a novelist.

CHAPTER 3

The Beginnings with Harper & Brothers

FROM 1835 to 1841, the prestigious Harper & Brothers firm of New York City published five of Ingraham's works. It was in these years that Ingraham's writing future was molded, and in these years he produced what must be regarded as his best work. The two-volume format was the norm in the era in which Ingraham wrote,[1] and all his Harper productions—one travel book and four novels—appeared in handsome two-volume duodecimo sets. Under the watchful eye of this established publisher, his works were also carefully proofread, were printed and bound with care, and were generally mechanically correct.

The two-volume format was good in that the author could (and did) plan to have the maximum space in which to develop his work; the convention was not such a positive factor when the writer's story was so thin that he had to resort to padding to fill out two volumes. Ingraham did pad at times, but, to his credit, the padding is minimal, and his Harper stories are generally well-sustained, although the twentieth-century critic would hardly regard them as organic wholes since there is material that could be omitted from all of them. The twentieth-century critic, it must be noted, would hardly recognize any pre-1850 novel as organic.

All but a handful of Ingraham novels are classified as romantic because they are marked by strong action scenes and because their episodes are based on love, adventure, and combat. Ingraham used elements from melodrama, the gothic novel, the sentimental novel, and the epistolary novel throughout his career, but since he was most often more concerned with action than with character, with what may have been more than actuality, he is considered a romantic novelist.

It appears to have been customary for writers of Ingraham's era to sell their copyrights to their publishers for a one-time fee at whatever price could be agreed upon. The publisher, then, could print a popular work repeatedly after the initial agreement was concluded and pay an author nothing after that initial agreement payment was fulfilled. Such seems to have been the case with Ingraham who, though a popular novelist, spent much of his life on the borderline of financial insolvency. He did not, or could not, demand and get control of the printing plates of his works as did Washington Irving and James Fenimore Cooper. Irving and Cooper, in effect, paid publishers a royalty to print some of their works and enjoyed, as a result, a much healthier economic life.[2] Could Ingraham have commanded such terms, he might have written less and been esteemed more by current audiences.

I The South-West

The South-West, written "By a Yankee" and published in 1835, was Ingraham's first book and his first success. Though published anonymously, as were all his Harper books, the author's identity was never a secret. A travel book, *The South-West's* two volumes detail the author's trip by sailing ship from New England to the Bahamas and Cuba to the mouth of the Mississippi River. At the mouth of the Mississippi he transferred to another ship that was towed to New Orleans by a steamship. He stayed in New Orleans and observed the sights a few weeks before he continued up the river to Natchez, Mississippi, from which point he traveled to various other Mississippi towns. Ingraham says in his introduction that the volumes "grew out of a private correspondence, which the author, at the solicitations of his friends, has been led to throw into the present form, modifying in a great measure the epistolary vein" (I, v). The two volumes, composed of forty-three letters or chapters, record the author's travels around 1830 and 1831. But before publication in 1835, Ingraham inserted several passages and footnotes to bring his readers up-to-date on the current status of some of the places and situations he saw.

The South-West is important not only as Ingraham's first work but also as a preview of things to come. It is a partial catalog of settings for future novels, and its romantic attitudes recur as does the author's penchant for details. Indeed, Ingraham's ability to

The Beginnings with Harper & Brothers 51

record even the tiniest details is one of his greatest strengths as a writer. His choice of the first-person point of view enables him to give his readers a sense of involvement, a real sense of participating in the activities he discusses. Some of Ingraham's flaws as a writer—stemming in part from the author's use of pretentious language—are also evident in *The South-West*.

Ingraham's ship left New England some time in November. In describing the voyage, he plunges almost at once into the rhetorical language of sentimental romanticism, and, at the same time, shows his eye for detail.

> As I stood beside the helmsman, I could feel the gallant vessel springing away from under me, quivering through every oaken nerve, like a high-mettled racer with his goal but a bound before him. As she encountered some more formidable wave, there would be a tremendous outlay of animal-like energy, a momentary struggle, a half recoil, a plunging, trembling—*onward* rush—then a triumphant riding over the conquered foe, scattering the gems from its shivered crest in glittering showers over her bows. Then gliding with velocity over the glassy concave beyond, swaying to its up-lifting impulse with a graceful inclination of her lofty masts, and almost sweeping the sea with her yards, she could majestically recover herself in time to gather power for a fresh victory. (I, 23)

Although the foregoing passage reveals some of Ingraham's stylistic predilections, the following description of landlubbers trying to walk on deck displays more readily the author's often unnecessary rhetoric:

> Our tyros of the sea, in their venturesome projections of their persons from one given point in their eye to another, in the hope of accomplishing a straight line, after vacillating most appallingly, would finally succeed "haud passibus aequis" in reaching the position aimed for, fortunate if a lee-lurch did not accommodate them with a dry bed in the "lee scuppers." (I, 21)

Besides Latin, the Professor also sprinkles French quotations throughout the book; such departures from English serve no positive purpose.

As Ingraham chronicles the progress of the ship, he also mentions many topics he would return to in his later fiction. He mentions Portland and its bay, Yankee chebacco boats and their fishermen, Bermuda, Cuba, the wreckers of the Bahamas, chivalrous buccaneers, revenue cutters, and an incident on the Plate River in 1827. After observing sugar plantations on the way up the Mississippi, the Professor arrives in New Orleans in December following a passage of little more than a month.

Over half of volume one is devoted to a description of 1830 New Orleans and its environs. Ingraham visits and describes the French Quarter, the coffeehouses, the Market, and various schools, theaters, convents, and churches. The exotic character of New Orleans appeals greatly to the young man, and he vividly describes the gambling "hells," the duels, and the handsome Creoles. Ingraham seems to have been an extremely open-minded traveler, yet he displays dashes of prudery when he comments on how many bars were available. He is impressed by the method of burial used in New Orleans and remarks that Northerners (to whom the volume was primarily addressed) might conserve land as well as improve the appearance of cemeteries if they were to bury their dead above ground in vaults. Ingraham commends the beauty of quadroons and watches two steamboats laden with bales of cotton light up the town as they burn at night. He visits the battlefield of New Orleans and a sugar plantation. He notices that New Orleans society is not as fixed or rigid as New England society, that the people are not as prescriptive as to what is right or wrong—all these things the Yankee traveler finds admirable. After a few weeks he leaves New Orleans and heads up the Mississippi, apparently most impressed with what he has observed and with the South in general.

The first chapter of volume 2 is devoted to Ingraham's river journey to Natchez, Mississippi, and the remaining nineteen are devoted to description and comments on Natchez and the surrounding towns and plantations. While New Orleans boasted plantations, Ingraham does not dwell on them as he does on the Southern plantation society of Natchez. He writes that "The society of Natchez, now, is not surpassed by any in America" (II, 50) and then proceeds to discuss the soil, the climate, the flora, and the Indian mounds as well as to give the customary descriptions of various public and private buildings.

Volume 2, more digressive and leisurely than its predecessor, describes Ingraham's initial trip and his five years' residence in Natchez as well as his deliberations on his adopted home, comments that any untraveled and prejudiced Yankee surely found instructive. He remarks frequently and informatively on the subject of slavery, and his comments, to his credit, are almost entirely without prejudice. Like most Northerners, Ingraham did not advocate slavery, but he did come to believe that Negroes were not intellectually ready for freedom. As he saw it, Southerners generally treated their slaves well, and almost indulgently; it was the Northern slaveholders who were most likely to be rough or brutal with their slaves.

Ingraham visits a slave market and finds buyers and sellers alike considerate, the buyers often buying the wife to please a purchased male slave. He notes the caste system in operation among the blacks, a system in which field hands are outranked by and cost less than house servants, who would not associate with their lower-class fellows. Slaves believed that to be sold quickly was a mark of their excellence and would serve faithfully their buyers. Edgar Allan Poe, also a Southerner, reviewed *The South-West* for the *Southern Literary Messenger* and commented that Ingraham's handling of slavery, his "strict honesty, impartiality, and unprejudiced common sense . . . [was] the most praiseworthy feature of his book." Poe continued by saying "future productions of the same author . . . [would] be looked for with anxiety" and noted that "A novelist of talent would find New Orleans the place of all places for the localities of a romance."[3] Ingraham did not let his newly acquired audience wait long, and he did set his next work, a romance, primarily in the environs of New Orleans.

II *The Byronic Lafitte*

Published in 1836, *Lafitte* was Ingraham's first novel and a financial success. Founded in small degree on the activities of Jean Lafitte at New Orleans in 1812, the work is an historical romance which owes something to Sir Walter Scott—who is credited with bringing the pirate into romantic literature in *Rokeby* (1813)[4]—and to Lord Byron's conception of the Byronic hero-villain. Indeed, Ingraham is credited with creating the first Byronic character in American historical romances.[5] The fusion of some fact with much fiction was, by Ingraham's time, a popular device that was an attempt to overcome the conventional objection that imaginative works were immoral.[6]

The link with Byron is acknowledged on the title page of *Lafitte* where Ingraham quotes from *The Corsair:* " 'He left a Corsair's name to other times,/ Link'd with one virtue and a thousand crimes' " (I, 3). The preface indicates the proportion of fact and fiction in the work: "With the pages of history . . . we have had to do, only so far as they could be made subservient to our tale" (I, 7).

The tale begins among the green hills of the Kennebec River in Maine. The twin brothers Achille and Henri, sons of an exiled French nobleman, are introduced on the day of their fifteenth birthday. Achille is tall, strong, passionate, and raven-haired; Henri is less tall, less strong, amiable, and has auburn hair. Achille discovers, by means of the father's birthday present, that his father loves his brother more and also plans to take Henri to Europe while Achille is sent off to college. Furious, Achille throws Henri against a marble pedestal which cuts a gash over the latter's left eyebrow. After some weeks, Henri recovers.

Four years pass, and Achille returns home with his college degree and discovers his father still prefers the fairer son. He also discovers they have brought home Gertrude Langueville, a cousin with whom Achille falls madly in love. When he finds that his love is not requited and that Henri and Gertrude have plighted troth, Achille knifes his brother and leaves home a fratricide.

The second section of the story opens fifteen years later in the bay of Barritaria, southwest of New Orleans; the bearded and mustachioed Lafitte is planning a raid on a rich man's home. A treacherous nephew leads Lafitte and his band to the home, where they are surprised and must fight their way back to the ship. To aid in his escape, Lafitte snatches the beautiful dark-haired Constanza Velasquez as a hostage and flees in his ship, the *Gertrude.* After Lafitte has gone, Count Alphonse D'Oyley, who is betrothed to Constanza, swears to catch the pirate of the gulf.

But Lafitte has loved Constanza at first sight, treats her well, and, at her request, releases her and guarantees her safe passage to Kingston, Jamaica, by sending with her his second in command, Theodore, and a black slave, Juana. The Kingston-bound ship is dismasted in a storm, and the survivors are picked up by one of Lafitte's armada which soon engages a French ship and takes D'Oyley prisoner. When Constanza and D'Oyley appear at Lafitte's stronghold, the chivalrous pirate agrees to set them both free presently, but D'Oyley mistrusts Lafitte and escapes with Constanza. Lafitte is furious, but Theodore talks the buccaneer into letting them keep their freedom.

After a week's interval the story begins again with a detailed description of Lafitte, his slave Cudjoe, and Lafon, a decrepit old man. An English ship comes into Barritaria and anchors under the guns of Lafitte's stronghold. The English captain has come to enlist Lafitte's help against America in the War of 1812 and offers him a captaincy and a chance at becoming respectable in the eyes of the world. Lafitte, a patriot in spite of his profession, says he will give the English an answer in two weeks and leaves immediately for New Orleans, where he sees Governor Claiborne and offers his services to America. Claiborne believes in Lafitte's sincerity, but the council of the city rejects the pirate's offer. They later recant, however, and Lafitte and his men do gallant service in the Battle of New Orleans where the pirate is severely wounded by an unprincipled British officer who takes advantage of Lafitte when he has stopped fighting. The buccaneer is nursed back to health in a convent, where he identifies a nun as Gertrude who recognizes him as Achille. Lafitte discovers that he is not a fratricide when Gertrude tells him that Henri is still alive.

The buccaneer and his men are pardoned by President Madison for their service in the Battle of New Orleans. Lafitte sails off to search for and apologize to his brother. On his way, he stops by his former fortress and finds Constanza there. She was kidnapped by Cudjoe at the demand of an African prophetess who was using the slave to get the woman for Martinez, one of Lafitte's captains who lusts for the lady. Cudjoe, however, saw through the plan and killed all concerned except Constanza, whom he marooned at the fortress with Juana. Lafitte promises to help her find D'Oyley, but it is D'Oyley who finds Lafitte. The Frenchman, finding Constanza gone, had put on an English uniform and wounded Lafitte at New Orleans. He catches up with Lafitte again at Havana and blasts off the masts of the ex-pirate's ship despite the white flag Lafitte raises. D'Oyley comes aboard and is soon in hand-to-hand combat with Lafitte, who keeps insisting that Constanza's honor is intact. But D'Oyley will not listen and runs Lafitte through. As the ex-pirate sinks to the deck, he recognizes Henri as his antagonist. Old Lafon also recognizes his son Henri, and, reunited with his family, Lafitte/

Achille dies in their arms. Gertrude remains in the convent and dies a nun.

Though it has flaws, there is much that is commendable about Ingraham's first novel. The Professor's portrayal of Lafitte is one of his best characterizations. Lafitte is truly Byronic; both a criminal and violent man, he suffers greatly from pangs of conscience and remorse. The internal conflict that gives Lafitte little rest is often well-expressed, and just as often melodramatic:

> "What matters it," he suddenly exclaimed, "that I have gained the wealth of princes—that I have waded through crime and blood to the acquisition of the guilty fame that makes my name terrible!—that my hand has been against every man!—I am at last but a miserable being—penitent, without the power to repent—remorseful, without hope—a lover of virtue, without daring to seek it—banned of God—outlawed of my race—fratricide, murderer! hundred-fold murderer! with the mark of Cain branded upon my brow, and burned deep—deep into my soul. Oh, God! oh, God!—if there be a God"—he cried, clasping his hands and lifting eyes to heaven—"be merciful unto my iniquities, for they are very great!" (I, 114)

Love for Gertrude led Achille to kill, and love for Constanza makes him change his life to the extent of fighting for the country he loved. The reader feels some pity when the Byronic hero-villain dies at the hand of his brother. D'Oyley wounded Lafitte unfairly at New Orleans; when he fights Lafitte again, he will not believe the ex-pirate's insistence that Constanza is safe and kills Lafitte in a rage. Lafitte cannot be glorified, but neither can the impetuous D'Oyley. Ingraham is adept though not masterly in his portrayal of the tormented Lafitte. The portrayal is, in some degree, a psychological one because the Professor did attempt to look at the reasons for Lafitte's actions. The author would draw other fine portraits of other obsessed Byronic hero-villains, but none surpasses Lafitte in its power and intensity.

Ingraham was among the first nineteenth-century authors to use the Negro as a character. Lafitte's slave Cudjoe and the female slave Juana, who aids Constanza, have prominent places in the story. Cudjoe

> was a young slave about four feet high, with a glossy black skin, ivory white teeth, two of which, flanking his capacious jaws, projected

outwards, with the dignity of the embryo tusks of a young elephant. His lips were of ample dimensions, and of the brightest vermillion, the lower one hanging down, and resting familiarly upon his short, retreating chin. . . .

His neck, short, thick, and bull-like, was set into broad shoulders, from which depended long arms hanging by his side like those of the ourang-outang and terminating in short stunted fingers, of which useful ornaments two and a half were wanting. (II, 35)

Cudjoe's grotesque appearance is not typical, but his faithfulness to his master is. "His natural disposition was gentle and affectionate" (II, 36), but he was not a man to cross. When he discovers he is being used by Oula the sorceress for Martinez's purposes, he kills Oula, her son, and Martinez.

Juana is presented as more of a type character than Cudjoe; her personality is not developed beyond the characteristics often attributed to Negro women. Her love, affection, and willingness to do anything necessary to aid Constanza are those qualities Ingraham emphasizes.

Ingraham, like Scott, is lavish in the description of his characters. Unfortunately, the Professor seems to have equated detailed description with characterization, and his characters are too often one-dimensional. Poe, in reviewing *Lafitte* for the *Southern Literary Messenger,* thought Ingraham had gone too far with those details. "Not a dog yelps, unsung [wrote Poe]. Not a shovel-footed negro waddles across the stage . . . without eliciting from the author a *vos plaudite*, with an extended explanation of the character of his personal appearance—of his length, depth, and breadth—and, more particularly, of the length, depth, and breadth of his shirt-collar, shoe buckles and hatband."[7]

Ingraham, again like Scott,[8] is similarly lavish in his depiction of setting. Such scenes as the opening vista of the Kennebec Valley in *Lafitte* and the later picture of the bay of Barritaria become set pieces; most Ingraham novels hereafter begin with a lengthy description of the setting in which some of the drama is to be enacted. Such scenes are built with care and are generally well done, though they are often forgotten after the players come upon the stage.

The language of these players constitutes a severe fault in *Lafitte:* that of the main character is too stilted, too full of ludicrous posturings and sentiments. Lafitte is almost impossibly good when he is in a noble mood but interesting and believable when his baser nature exercises its influence. It is the minor characters—Cudjoe, Juana, and the Dutchman Getzendanner—who speak most naturally and without heroic affectation; and they speak in dialect. Such believability acts as a partial corrective to the flatness of the characterizations. In most of Ingraham's work, the characters who speak in dialect speak more naturally than anyone else.

Another fault of the novel, and one which is certainly the mark of a less than superior novelist, is the disunity of the plot; it is too open. The movement of the characters is too easy to guess, the foreshadowing too obvious. To Ingraham's credit, however, the directness in the portrayal of activity has a physical strength that does hold the reader's attention.

That *Lafitte* held the reader's attention is testified to by the book's sales, its frequent reprintings,[9] and Louisa Medina's play based on it; Ingraham was on his way up in the literary ranks. He had successfully attempted an American-based travel book and a novel based solidly in America. He did not stray far from America and Americans in his next novel.

III A Romance of the American Revolution

Burton; or, The Sieges (1838) purports to be a tale of the early youth of Aaron Burr and his involvement in the American Revolution. The sieges of the title are the military sieges of Quebec and New York, which form the subplot, and the personal sieges laid by Burton against the chastity of three young ladies, which form the main plot.

Burton is a "fascinating libertine" (II, 266), and his character and that of the three women in the story are worthy of comment as type characters—weak blond ones and strong dark ones. Burton is the black-haired, black-eyed, ambitious Byronic hero-villain. Caroline Germaine has brown hair, blue eyes, and a pale complexion. She is seduced by Burton, and, when abandoned for another, dies of a broken heart like a proper sentimental heroine. Isabel Ney, with black hair and eyes, is also seduced by Burton. But she, a stronger, more ambitious woman, shoots and wounds Burton when he is on the verge of abandoning her. The third female object of siege, Eugenie de Lisle, is auburn-haired; she loves Burton also, but rejects his improper advances, banishes him when she learns his true nature, and is rewarded for her purity. The weak blondes and strong dark characters are found in almost every Ingraham novel. These types were obviously not original with him since many earlier authors had also used them.

The novel is very straightforward in organization and presentation of action. Burton, who is not named until the reader is two hundred pages into the novel, is traveling to Quebec through the valley of the Chaudiere River in November, 1775. He has been sent by Colonel Benedict Arnold to take news of the British movements in Canada to General Montgomery who, after several military successes, is marching on Quebec. The first two hundred pages of volume 1, those detailing Burton's journey, are the most tightly organized in all of Ingraham's work. Burton is in a hurry, and the story moves at a fast pace as it follows the protagonist meeting friends of the Revolution and being led by a motley assortment of Canadian guides through the wilderness. On his trip, Burton rescues Eugenie de Lisle from a convent where she has been imprisoned by a designing uncle. Burton leaves her under Montgomery's care and fights with the general in the ill-fated assault on Quebec in which the Americans are routed and Burton taken prisoner. Escaping from Sir Guy Carleton with Eugenie's aid, Burton and his youthful Canadian friend Zacharie Nicolet escape to New York where they rejoin the colonial forces.

In New York, in 1776, Burton seduces Caroline Germaine and then makes his first overtures to Isabel Ney, the daughter of a British officer. Eugenie, after several months, shows up at General Washington's house in search of her beloved Burton. Burton, in a less than brilliant move, gets Eugenie to nurse the dying, guilty, broken-hearted Caroline. Through Caroline and Colonel Arden, Eugenie learns of Burton's true character and renounces him over the dead body of Germaine. The love plot is now interrupted by the battle of New York, in which Burton distinguishes himself even though the British win another victory. Though the Americans lose, Burton triumphs over Isabel Ney. She swears revenge, however, when apprised of Burton's treatment of Caroline and Eugenie. She sets a trap for Burton in which British soldiers are to capture him, but, when that fails, shoots him through the shoulder. As Burton is borne on a litter to a doctor, he passes the lighted house of Washington and sees

Eugenie marry Arden. The seducer bites his lip until it bleeds, tries to rise with sword in hand, but weakly sinks back upon the litter and faints with a curse on his lips.

The novel was surely written with both aesthetic and didactic ends in mind. It is the most finished, artistically, of Ingraham's novels. Even the one or two episodes that digress from the plot are well-handled. The moral is obvious: the seducer's lot is not a happy one; evil will be justly rewarded. The novel breaks off with Burton on his litter, and we are supposed to be able to understand better how Burr, in later years, became "the Catiline of his country" (I, ix).

The character portrait of Burton's aide Zacharie Nicolet is one of the best in the novel. Zacharie is a fifteen-year-old Canadian who guides Burton on his way to Quebec and who serves him faithfully afterward. Saucy, precocious, full of dislike for orders and full of a love for giving them, Zacharie follows Burton because Burton trusts and respects him and does not treat the youngster as if he were fifteen.

One other short character vignette worthy of mention is that of Joseph Gerret, who rents a room to several men who plan to kidnap Washington. Gerret lives in wretched poverty but has a chest of gold and silver under his bed; he wears rags and patched clothing yet clips coins at night to add to his treasure. As other novels will show, Ingraham was fascinated with wealthy people and the ways they got or retained their money—possibly because he was almost always in financial want.

To obtain the "Invisibility and ubiquity" (II, 263) which are the novelist's proper attributes, Ingraham wrote his story from the subjective third-person omniscient point of view, the point of view he most often adopted. Occasionally the author did comment on the progress of the story. These tongue-in-cheek lines explain why Eugenie did not kill herself when she discovered Burton's faithlessness:

It would, no doubt, have been very fine for Eugenie to have stabbed herself with her dagger, like a true heroine of romance, when she became convinced of her lover's perjury. . . . But, considerate reader! there existed one or two obstacles to this. The first and foremost was, that we are drawing Eugenie from life, and, the truth is, she did not come to the tragic end aforesaid. The second, and, perhaps, equally forcible, is, that we should give you only a volume and a half of matter, whereas we are bound to our publishers to produce two respectable duodecimos, of neither less than two hundred and sixteen pages each nor more than two hundred and eighty-eight. (II, 221)

As noted, Ingraham's plot extension did not lose the reader. Indeed, Eugenie's living to be rewarded for her chastity is more believable than Caroline's dying at the feet of her lover.

Burton's character is more believable than Lafitte's; he is more human than heroic and does not stride through the novel sounding impossibly chivalric one moment and impossibly sentimental the next. He is an excellent, honorable soldier and gains fame for his exploits; even his human failing—lust—adds to the believability of his portrayal. Caroline is the most unbelievable character; she reads *The Sorrows of Werter* and sighs like a conventional sentimental heroine, sins in a summerhouse, and for that sin dies of a broken heart. Isabel Ney is completely believable as the avenging scorned woman, and equally impressive is the naive, but strong, Eugenie de Lisle. Taken as a whole, the characters in *Burton* are the most convincing in all of Ingraham's works.

The novel is more unified than most of his because the actions of Burton in love are reinforced and blended with the actions of war. Steady action holds the book together; though the plot is undeniably episodic and not organically unified, the pace seldom flags, and the reader's attention does not wander.

Though *Burton* is Ingraham's best novel in many respects, he was paid only $750 for it as compared to $1,350 he received for *Lafitte*.[10] Good as *Burton* was, a pirate was more popular, and Ingraham returned to another legendary buccaneer for his next tale.

IV The Wizard of the Sea

Captain Kyd (1839), a more complex novel than *Burton*, is peopled with a large number of characters who appear under different names at fortuitous intervals. Because of this complexity, there is an aura of confusion that pervades the novel, even to its fantastic closing scene.

Kyd opens at Castle Cor on the southern coast of Ireland in May, 1694, and concludes five years later in the colony of New York when Kyd is returned to England to be hanged. Ingraham again took what he needed from the pages of history to build his novel—Kyd (the real pirate spelled his name Kidd) did make his home in New York and did die in 1701.[11] This time, however, Ingraham allowed his imagination too much free rein. The greater part of the story takes place in Ireland, for it explains how Kyd started on his life of piracy. As the novel opens, an archery contest is being held on the lawn of Castle Cor in celebration of Kate Bellamont's sixteenth birthday. Kate, the dark heroine, wins her own contest and gives the prize, a silver arrow, to her fair-haired esquire and lover Robert Lester. One of Kate's arrows was loosed at a hawk that happened to get into range, and the stricken hawk flutters over a nearby cliff with the arrow in him. At the risk of his life, Mark Meredith, a dark-haired fisherman's son who loves the proud Kate, descends the cliff to retrieve the hawk. His peril gives Kate's highborn cousin Grace Fitzgerald some alarm.

Robert, after some prodding, goes after the lowborn Mark, but Mark is too proud to owe his life to Robert and jumps into the sea when he cannot return up the cliff without Lester's help. Mark swims to shore, walks back with the hawk, and gives it to Kate, but his proud bearing irritates Robert, who grabs the young servant by the throat. Mark throws him down, and Lester hurls a spear at him but misses his target. Kate is incensed at this conduct and banishes Robert from her presence. Kate, who is truly in love with Lester, cries because her lover has acted so unnobly, and, at Grace's urging, later sends a locket to Robert to show that he is forgiven his murderous inclinations. Grace takes the locket to Mark and asks him to deliver it. She tells Mark that he can win honor and thus rise from his lowly position; it is obvious to all but Mark that she loves the young fisherman.

Robert, after quitting Castle Cor, rides madly homeward and soon runs into the deformed witch Elpsy, who tells the highborn noble a tale calculated to humble him. There was a fisherman's daughter, she tells Robert, who was seduced by the pirate Hurtel of the Red Hand. When her bastard was born, Hurtel tried to put it to death. The fisherman's daughter, however, switched her son with that of a highborn lady, and Hurtel threw the noble infant off a tower into the ocean. But the baby's clothes caught on a rock, and the fisherman's daughter, attempting to rescue him, was likewise hurled from the tower. Her spine was injured in the fall, but she saved the child and gave it to her father to raise. The

The Beginnings with Harper & Brothers

lowborn bastard was raised as a noble, the highborn child as a fisherman. The lowborn bastard is, of course, Robert, and Elpsy's tale maddens the proud young man. He decides to follow in his father's ways and that very night joins the crew of a pirate ship that has conveniently anchored off the coast.

Mark, meanwhile, also meets Elpsy as he goes to deliver the locket. Elpsy tries to kill him, and, when Mark outwits her, gives him gold to leave the country; Mark needs little urging as he has already determined to make a worthy name for himself on the sea. He ships on an English vessel which is carrying Grace and Kate's father, the earl of Bellamont, to England. A hurricane hits the ship, and it is only through Mark's courage that the vessel is saved. The storm washes Grace overboard, but Mark saves her also. When the hurricane blows itself out, pirates attack the ship.

The fight between the pirates and the English crew is the best narrated, most realistic, and most richly detailed battle in all of Ingraham's novels. Heads fly; limbs are struck off, and people are generally dispatched in a masterful, gripping, gory melee. One group of the pirates, as might be expected, is led by Lester, who is unrecognized because the fight takes place at night. Mark has killed the pirate chief while protecting Grace but is so severely wounded that he falls. When Lester, who takes full command of the pirates at the death of their captain, sees Grace, his love for her prevents him from allowing the pirates to harm her, and the buccaneers retreat to their ship though they have won the battle.

The story now breaks in the middle for a five-year lapse before it resumes in the colony of New York which is now governed by the earl of Bellamont. Captain Kyd, in a ship named *The Silver Arrow*, is ravaging the coast. Elpsy, transported from Ireland as an undesirable character, now lives at Hellgate near New York. Captain Rupert Fitzroy, in his ship the *Ger-Falcon*, is searching the coast for Kyd when he is not wooing Kate Bellamont who has promised to marry him. Fitzroy's secretary, mustachioed Edwin Gerald, is devotedly attached to his captain to whom he tells a tale of past unrequited love. Lester suddenly visits Kate and declares his never-dimmed passion for her, but she knows he is Kyd and spurns him though it is obvious she still loves him. From her, Kyd learns Fitzroy is his rival, and he leaves vowing to kill him. He does catch up with Fitzroy, sees him drown in the sea, and returns to take Kate to Ireland and claim his lands as lord of Lester. But Kate shoots him in the arm, and Kyd leaves. Fitzroy, meanwhile, has survived and learned that Kate still loves Kyd. He then goes after the pirate, captures, and imprisons him.

Kate visits Lester in prison the night before sentence is to be passed on him. A certain Father Nanfan sneaks up on them and pronounces them man and wife as they are kneeling together. On the next day all the threads of the novel are tied up in a hasty series of events that is more characteristic of the short novels Ingraham later wrote than of his Harper productions. Elpsy reveals that the Kyd is Lester, that Fitzroy is Mark Meredith and the true lord of Lester, and that Father Nanfan is Hurtel of the Red Hand. Hurtel kills his estranged wife for her revelations. Kate is now married to Kyd, but the earl of Bellamont still sends the pirate to England to be executed; Kate dies of a broken heart. Edwin is discovered to be the disguised Grace Fitzgerald, and she and Mark are eventually married.

A brief summary such as the above does not reveal by any means all the complexities of Ingraham's plot, but it does serve to illustrate the important facets of it: the familiar light and dark heroes and heroines, the motif of the name switch, and the device of two young men who love the same maiden and who are separated in youth to clash again climactically in manhood. Grace's masquerading as a man is an old plot device but one new to Ingraham. As in *Lafitte*, the Professor has tried to explain how the highborn Lester became the ferocious Kyd, thus palliating to some extent the deeds to which the pirate was driven, and, as in *Burton*, one of the heroines shoots the Byronic hero-villain Kyd.

Had Ingraham chosen to weave a less complex tale he might have produced a better one. The witch Elpsy is a case in point, for Ingraham made her carry much of the burden of the novel. She comes through well as the wronged fisher's daughter who wishes her son to be the lord of Lester and who wants revenge on her seducer, but she does not get her wish or her revenge. Presumably, as a witch, she is supposed to be regarded as a gothic character capable of inspiring horror, but she is a very poor witch and, actually, a fraud. She sprinkles various colorful elements into fires, but she works no witchcraft and gets all her information from personal experience or from people too terrified of the hunchbacked woman to refuse the answers she demands. Her wild appearance and red hair make the superstitious fear and obey her, but she is really a woman to be more pitied than feared.

The unequal development of the novel also works against it. Three-fifths of it is devoted to the scenes in Ireland, the preparation for Kyd's career, but Kyd as a pirate appears only briefly; his piratical exploits are told by various Dutchmen who discuss Kyd's activities. *Lafitte* at least gives a fuller picture of the matured pirate. The weakest part of *Captain Kyd* remains its abrupt ending in which too many revelations are thrust upon the reader too hurriedly. The careful reader is not surprised by all these revelations, but their precipitate manner is quite at variance with the leisurely development of the rest of the novel.

With all its faults, *Kyd* remains readable today, though it has little historical or intrinsic value. Its one genuine excellence—the superbly written battle between the pirates and the English ship—is worth waiting for, and, in many ways, it is the climax of the novel. Ingraham's swift narration keeps the story moving, but the five-year break after the fight injures the novel, and it never really regains its momentum after that.

Ingraham received $1,200 for the copyright to *Kyd*, making the payment second only to the $1,350 he received for *Lafitte*.[12] *Kyd*, then, was a financial success, and the version of it dramatized for the stage by Joseph Stevens Jones was also a success, as judged by its performance record.[13] From current perspectives it was perhaps unfortunate that *Kyd* was so popular, since it was not one of Ingraham's best. The Professor evidently believed that the devices used in the novel—improbable coincidences, breaks in the action, characters with a mysterious knowledge of the past, endings that neatly dispose of every character—would continue to insure financial success. Many of his future novels were financially successful, but, from a critical standpoint, the novels from *Captain Kyd* onward were more derivative than original, written more for the masses than for the discriminating reader.

V *Back to the Southwest*

Ingraham's fourth romance and fifth work, *The Quadroone; or, St. Michael's Day*, was printed by Harper in 1841. The novel had been written earlier and printed in London in 1840; the first chapter of it appeared in the November, 1839, *United States*

Magazine, and Democratic Review.[14] *The Quadroone* was his last novel published by Harper and must be considered the worst even though its Byronic hero-villain, Garcia Ramarez, the count of Osma, is wicked enough to hold the reader's attention. The novel contains an early treatment of the evils produced by miscegenation;[15] the lovely quadroone for whom the tale is named is almost the victim of incest.

The action opens in New Orleans in June, 1766, when a small band of Spanish soldiers led by the count of Osma enters the city and demands that the French province be surrendered to the laws of Spain. Predictably, the French loyalists resist, and only the enraged Osma escapes back to his ship. The resistance to the Spanish is ably led by Renault the Quadroon, the illegitimate son of the marquis of Caronde, who is the governor of New Orleans. Renault cuts down the Spanish flag when Osma attempts to raise it; his sister Azèlie (the quadroone of the novel's title) catches the flag, cuts it into eight pieces, and is wounded by Osma for her patriotism. For his bravery and his leadership in the fight against the Spanish, the young men of the city decide to overlook Renault's heritage and call him friend.

The quadroon (male) or quadroone (female), according to Ingraham, has four parts of white blood to one part of Negro. A quadroon at the time of this tale was regarded as a slave; the males were regarded as almost useless and allowed to roam freely about while the women were reared to become the mistresses of rich white men. Marriage with a white was forbidden. The people of New Orleans accepted this system of concubinage, and no mention of change is breathed during the course of the novel.

Both Renault and Azèlie are understandably bitter about their heritage; neither of them has a last name as slaves did not, and both are bastards as well as slaves. Both are black-haired, black-eyed, proud individuals admired for their form and beauty. Renault swears to protect his sister's chastity and to see her dead before she becomes a mistress to whomever their mother Ninine might decide to sell her; Azèlie even carries a dagger in her bosom to kill herself with should her innocence be endangered.

Osma returns in the early autumn of 1769, over three years after his abortive attempt to take over New Orleans. By this time even the French loyalists know that France has given New Orleans to Spain, but a few of the city's natives still oppose giving

The Beginnings with Harper & Brothers

up their city, and there is another fight before Osma finally becomes governor. In that fight, a young Spanish noble, Don Henrique, is wounded; a tall, mysterious woman tells Renault to save him, and the quadroon takes the wounded cavalier home for Azèlie to nurse in opulent oriental surroundings. Azèlie and Henrique fall in love at first sight. Osma, who has arrived with his beautiful daughter Estelle, is so enraged at Henrique's disappearance that he gives his men orders to burn New Orleans to the ground. But the mysterious woman appears to him, has him countermand his order, and tells him that he will pay for his sins on St. Michael's Day, September 29.

Osma, however, is not through with sinning. He plots to kill the deposed French councillors, and volume 1 ends with his machinations almost fulfilled. Estelle suspects her father's intentions and tells her fears to Renault who saves the councillors and spares Osma at Estelle's request. Estelle and Renault fall in love. Renault, in one of several soliloquies, gives some indication of the mental torture he suffers because of his fate:

> "But what have I, an accursed quadroon—I, to do with a maiden's love like her? Like the worshippers of the sun, I may adore her afar off till blinded by my devotion, and my heart is burned up by her unapproachable brightness. Alas! for what do I live? wherefore do I court life? From this hour death is most welcome! Why did Heaven give me a heart to love, and then link me with a race to whom love is forbidden?" (II, 17)

Estelle is somewhat worried at being in love with a quadroon herself but is relieved when the mysterious woman later tells her that Renault is as noble and freeborn as herself.

Meanwhile, Ninine arranges to sell Azèlie's charms to Osma for ten thousand crowns. When Osma learns Henrique loves Azèlie, he has Henrique chained in the deepest dungeon available to await execution at the governor's whim. Osma soon recaptures six of the seven French councillors and has them executed. He takes Azèlie to his quarters and prepares to violate her despite something uneasily familiar in her countenance. He brings Henrique out of the dungeon to see the helpless Azèlie in his power. The quadroone, however, is saved by the mysterious woman who tells the count that his claim to Azèlie and Renault (whom his mother has given Osma as a slave) will be tested in a tribunal on St. Michael's Day, and that he is to forbear his passion until then. Because of his guilty conscience, Osma is scared of the woman, and he agrees to do as she orders. The woman later rescues Henrique, and the little group awaits its fate.

On St. Michael's Day justice is served by a spate of revelations that must surely rank as one of the most fantastically coincidental scenes on record. The mysterious woman reveals that Renault is the true son of the marquis of Caronde; Ninine has switched her bastard with the legitimate son of the nobleman. The illegitimate son, Jules, later breaks his mother's neck. Azèlie, the mysterious woman continues, is Osma's daughter from an earlier marriage than the one that produced Estelle. The mysterious woman herself is shown to be the faithful servant of Azèlie's dead mother. An Indian chief, Ihuahua, appears and reveals he is Osma's brother, a brother Osma thought he had killed long ago. Henrique is revealed as heir to the throne of Spain. Osma, enraged and terrified by the retribution that will be his, throws himself on his sword in front of everyone. Azèlie, no longer a quadroone, marries Henrique but dies before he becomes king of Spain. Renault marries Estelle.

Though the novel is marred by its *deux ex machina* ending, it boasts several excellent character portrayals. The best is that of Garcia Ramarez, the evil and guilty count of Osma. His wickedness, hatred, and vindictiveness are enhanced by his stature and commanding presence. He shows no sign of repentance or contrition as he lusts for a young girl who proves to be his daughter. Osma wants to appear fair and just in the world's eyes so that he may continue to rise in the estimation of his Spanish superiors. To keep up such a front, he uses assassins against those standing in the way of his ambitions. Estelle wants to believe there is some good in her father and, in trying to convince herself, gives one definition of the Byronic hero-villain her father is: " 'He hath virtues with his crimes. . . . No man is altogether bad—no one so wholly wicked that he hath not some redeeming quality that invites love and confidence. How else is it that the darkest bandit and most ferocious outlaw have ever found woman's affection to entwine itself around their rugged hearts?' " (I, 243).

Another memorable character, and one of a quite different sort, is Gobin, the fool in motley. Gobin is more fool than masquerader, more a natural clown than a pretended one. His conversation with the Spanish cavalier Garcilaso is representative. Gobin has the French emblems of office—the state seal and keys—and Garcilaso is trying to bribe the fool into giving them up for a chain of silver bells:

"Then quit them, wise fool!"
"Thou hast well said 'wise fool!' My folly would make me put my neck in reach o' thy sword for that tinkling chain, whereas my wisdom keepeth me here in safety. Wisdom causeth me to lose my chain, so that my folly cause me not to lose my head!"
"I'faith, thou art both logical and wise, fool," answered the cavalier.
"Marry, then, gossip, I'll tell thee a secret! 'Twas the weight o' logic that cracked my brain, and folly jumped in at the hole. Wisdom hath patched it up o' the outside, but, as thou see'st, has made but sorry work at it." (I, 52)

Gobin contributes the only humor or light conversation to be found in *The Quadroone*. Since everyone else is either deadly serious or seriously heroic, Gobin's verbal interludes, with their Shakespearean echoes, are all the more welcome.

The rest of the characters are not fully rounded human beings. Renault, the hero, is full of chivalric noble ideas about protecting his sister; that protection, in fact, is all he lives for until Estelle is introduced. When Renault is not being heroic, he is condemning his lot as a quadroon. The reader sympathizes with Renault's situation but cannot care greatly about Renault as a person because Renault is too heroic or too abject to be believable. Much the same thing is wrong with Azèlie.

The novel received mixed reviews. Poe, writing in *Graham's*, was ashamed of it, but the reviewer for the *Ladies' Companion* not only liked it but thought Ingraham was "destined to become one of the most popular novelists of America."[16] Ingraham was already one of the most popular novelists of the day, and his star was to continue to rise—but not with the firm of Harper & Brothers.

Ingraham had proposed, in 1839, to deliver two novels a year to the Harpers for which he was to be paid a total of $3,000. He did not get half that much for his 1839 *Captain Kyd*, and it is not known if he received over six hundred dollars for *The Quadroone*.[17] The uncertainty about his payment was, understandably, a source of irritation for the author. His impatience was evident when he wrote Fletcher Harper on January 31,

1840, that he wanted either to know definitely when he was going to receive the nine hundred dollars due him on *The Quadroone* or to have permission "to make a disposition of the ms elsewhere." Ingraham also commented that "I only regret that I cannot act more independently."[18] The time to act independently was upon him, for *The Quadroone* was the last novel Harper published. The above letter and others to the firm indicate that the parting of author and publisher was mutually agreed upon with little rancor on either side. Fletcher Harper's acceptance of five short stories published in *Harper's New Monthly Magazine* from 1856 through 1858 suggests that he harbored few bad feelings.

The five books published by Harper & Brothers are a good introduction to the writings of Joseph Holt Ingraham. They display his predilection for stories with largely American settings, for stories of the sea, and for stories based in some degree in American history. All of his Harper books display his penchant for romantic elements and his ability to employ much detail. *The South-West, Lafitte,* and *Burton* are the best of the five and show that Ingraham could write well, that he could create suspense effectively, and that he could keep the reader's interest. Padding is not foreign to these works, but it is minimal, and the works do show that some care and planning went into their composition. Lack of care, lack of planning, and too much padding became obvious in many of the works produced after 1841. Ingraham was not satisfied in all respects with Harper & Brothers, but time would show that he was not to be totally satisfied elsewhere either.

CHAPTER 4

Five Years and Eighty Novels

FROM 1842 through 1847 Ingraham produced at least eighty novels published in paper covers; they ranged in length from thirty to over one hundred finely printed double-columned pages. The main printers of these novels were Edward P. and Henry L. Williams of Boston, who issued books under several imprints—E. P. Williams, Edward P. Williams, H. L. Williams, Henry L. Williams, Williams, Williams and Brothers, Williams Brothers, and the "Yankee" Office—from their Congress Street address. Perhaps because most of these five years were spent in the North, Ingraham often used the settings of metropolitan Boston, New York, or Philadelphia for some of the action; novels based in the South for this period are few.

Of the stories Ingraham wrote during these years, the largest number were tales of pirates and of the sea. Stories of the city or of the differences in the city and the country made up the second largest group. There were also tales of the "American Dream," narratives of the Revolutionary War and the War of 1812, a few novels of the various social ills he had observed in America, and tales without American settings. Most of them have a love story for a main plot or subplot, but they do not all have happy endings.

In order to get these novels printed, Ingraham was required to pare them down from the two-volume format he had been using. Many of them, in fact, seem to have been limited to ten chapters like *The Dancing Feather* (1842), the first of the eighty. *Morris Graeme,* the 1843 sequel to *The Dancing Feather,* has an introduction that indicates the author's feelings about this limitation:

> It was the original intention of the author of the "Dancing Feather" to have extended that work to fifty chapters, or the usual length of a

novel of two volumes. But the editor of the paper to whom it was communicated in weekly numbers, requested, after six chapters had been published, that it should be limited to ten chapters. This desire of the publisher the author complied with, though with injury both to the plot and the harmonious construction of the Romance. (3)

Statements like this one are printed in over a dozen novels; perhaps such statements were intended to forestall criticism of the author's lack of "harmonious construction" in these romances.

Since Ingraham had to abbreviate his paper-covered novels and because he rebelled against such shortening, these works are very often uneven in development. Typically, a novel moves along at a relatively even pace until the last chapter when a crowded conclusion occurs so suddenly that it is obvious the work could have been better planned. The novels of this period were written too hurriedly and with little or no revision. Typographical errors abound. In one instance, the name of the heroine changed in the course of the novel. Both Ingraham and his printers must share the blame for these avoidable annoyances.

The number of the novels and the frequency of their publication were factors that help explain why they were generally ignored by the critics. Another reason might be that, after a while, the novels began to appear very similar because Ingraham was stretching his limited talent too thin and reusing some of the same plots and character types. A novel of this period like *Rafael* (1845) typically begins with a panorama of a certain scene. The characters are then introduced with several paragraphs of description before the action begins. The action progresses for a chapter or two, at which point the narrative switches back to a time prior to the present action to show how the current state of affairs came about. After a few chapters of flashback, the story returns to the present and moves swiftly through a climax to a conclusion.

To this often predictable, though unorthodox, organization Ingraham would add one-dimensional character types, characters not fully developed, that soon became familiar. The young men are single, proud, tall, symetrically proportioned, and have black or brown hair. The description of Charles Blackford is typical:

> He was about twenty-two years of age, and . . . was of manly height and person. His forehead was high, white, blue-veined, and shaded with short brown hair. . . . The features were regular and strong. . . . His eyes were large and full of intellect, and the shape and fixedness of the mouth gave indication of energy, which the pervading softness of the eye qualified with the promise of great sensibility. The general expression of his face . . . was that of a frank and generous, but sensitive and proud spirit.[1]

The women are unmarried, young, less tall, physically well-rounded, and have either black or brown hair. For example, Biddy Woodhull of *Biddy Woodhull* (1844)

> was just seventeen and a perfect rustic beauty! Her hair was a dark brown, and curled beautifully all about her brows and adown her rounded neck. Her eyes were black and piercing, in the depths of which love unfledged, lay covert. Her lips were pliant coral, richly contrasting the beautiful setting of her pearly teeth which were displayed by the brightest and most beaming smile in the world—a smile that emanated from a glad pure heart and bold brow—and bright was the sun of the soul within to shine forth so radiantly upon the face. . . . all the charms of womanhood were ripening in her person—the eloquent eye, the modest walk, the subdued smile, with the sweetly full bust, and rounded waist, and symmetrical foot, all betrayed that the spring of womanhood was just deepening into the warm and glowing summer. . . . She was a girl of good sense, but of a high spirit. (4)

In their detail and length these portraits of a hero and a heroine are also typical.

If the characters are morally good, they are almost perfect. Henry Hayward of *The Dancing Feather* endures starvation and deprivation rather than join a group of wealthy pirates. If a character is immoral, he will come to a bad end, particularly if he has experimented with sex like Walter Blake of *Eleanor Sherwood* (1844). A few unmarried characters like Richard Berkeley of *Berkeley* (1846), however, are allowed to reform if they have not become sexually knowledgeable.

To these almost sterotyped characters are added other stock characters that appear in various novels. Male Jews, for instance, are always depicted as sharp-nosed moneylenders—as is Jacob Goldschnapp in *The Gipsy of the Highlands* (1843). Goldschnapp was a

> small, thin man, about fifty years of age. . . . His head was large . . . and covered with thick, black hair, slightly mixed with gray. His

forehead was high and retreating, and his eyebrows arched. His dark eyes were narrow-lidded and almond-shaped, and were restless and sharp. His nose was long, high set, and curving over the upper lip like the beak of an eagle. He had a heavy beard, which was shaved only about the mouth, which feature was thin-lipped, and expressive of avarice. A black, oily, silk cap was stuck on the top of his head, the tassel of which dangled over his left ear. (17)

Negroes appear often as family or body servants. They are frequently portrayed as dull individuals, but they are usually good people because they are always faithful to their masters. Buttermilk, in *The Surf Skiff* (1847), is also described as being a "paunch-bellied African Falstaff" (24). Dutchmen appear occasionally in the novels as either soldiers or merchants. One soldier is stout Slems Von Vow of *Leisler* (1846). Slems, like most of the Dutch characters, is rotund, benevolent, and speaks with a heavy dialect. An examination of the varied contexts in which all these character types appear will illustrate that Ingraham used plot types as well as character types.

I *Tales of Pirates and of the Sea*

The Dancing Feather, which appeared in 1842, marked the beginning of a new phase in the author's career. It was Ingraham's first brief novel and his first novel not published by Harper. The *Dancing Feather* is a ship manned by amateur pirates who occasionally plunder another vessel in order to be able to live like gentlemen in New York City. The captain of the pirates, George Carleton, explains to one of his victims that

"we are all young men who have been educated to be gentlemen without the birth or the fortune to sustain and maintain the rank of such. We entered the world and found it already apportioned to the laborious [sic] and the useful. We could not, therefore, but carve our fortunes out of it with such instruments as fortune had given us—and these were only our wits. We tried them on honesty, but they grew dull and blunted—we could not starve and mother earth refusing to nourish us, we threw ourselves upon the charity of father Neptune. When he has been generous to us we leave his domain awhile, and live like pleasant gentlemen on shore—till empty purses drive us once more to depend on his bounty. We are but amateur bucaniers!" (30)

The tale concerns the efforts of Morris Graeme, one of the pirates, to talk Henry Hayward, the hero, into joining the group. Henry, who has come to New York from Harvard, has no money, no job, and no friends. He saves dark-haired Catherine Powell from drowning, and the two fall in love at first sight, but, since Henry is poor, he leaves Catherine after he has rescued her. In his search for a job, Henry meets George Frederick Cooke Sykes, the memorable "universal genious" (15) who speaks a comic Shakespearean English and whom Henry sees die of starvation. Henry is jailed for stealing food but is freed after Graeme pays his bill. Graeme again attempts to get Henry to join the crew, but Henry still refuses. He soon falls from hunger and, providentially, is seen by Colonel Powell, Catherine's father. Henry recovers and is married to Catherine. Colonel Powell buys the *Dancing Feather* after the pirates are dispersed, but the buccaneers return and steal the ship. Word later comes that the *Feather* has been sunk in a battle with a Mexican sloop.

Neither *Feather* nor its sequel *Morris Graeme* is particularly memorable, but they do utilize the characters Ingraham had learned the public was interested in—pirates. Both stories suffer from lack of planning. The only thing that *Graeme* adds to the story is more detail as to how Carleton and Graeme became pirates. The "universal genious" is the only believable character; the others are either too good or too inconsistent for credibility. *The Dancing Feather* did, however, have enough action and enough love interest to sell twenty thousand copies and to excite some unknown playwright to dramatize it.[2]

Probably to capitalize on the success of *Lafitte*, Ingraham wrote an 1844 sequel, *Theodore*, to his first best-seller. Theodore, Lafitte's second-in-command, was taken in by Count D'Oyley and Constanza at the conclusion of the earlier novel. The sequel begins with several pages about Theodore quoted from *Lafitte* to orient the reader and then plunges into an account of Theodore's life after the death of Lafitte. Theodore is English and, when he was seven, was plucked from the wreckage of a ship by Lafitte. The young man knows nothing of his parentage. During the course of the novel he discovers he is of noble blood, becomes the earl of Clarence, marries well, and lives happily ever after. The idea of having a young man discover he is the heir to an English title and estates is a device that Ingraham employed more than once.

Another tale about the pirate Kidd is *The Spanish Galleon* (1845). It is not a sequel to *Captain Kyd*, does not mention the earlier novel, and even has Kidd meet a slightly different end. The only interesting thing about the novel is that Ingraham has Kidd's lieutenant, Belfort, sail to a monastery and demand the freedom of a maiden held captive by evil priests. Belfort not only did not know the girl but he also had no way of knowing she was a prisoner—facts Ingraham glosses over as his plot reaches its romantic conclusion.

Howard (1843) is the narrative of a young man who goes to sea to forget an unfortunate love affair. The impetus under which Howard leaves home is not unusual in an Ingraham story, and the novel offers the philosophy that going to sea is one of the best things a man can do: "If he is true, to himself he will make for himself a name. If half of the young men in shops would go to sea before the mast, they would make better members of society, and ennoble their own natures. . . . At sea men learn no vices" (6). This type of sentiment appears in different guises in several other novels of the sea, one of which is *The Midshipman* (1844).

The Midshipman is the tale of Frank Winters who joins the Navy, shoots an officer in a duel, resigns, and then goes to Marseilles where he loses most of his mother's fortune. In a well-narrated, suspenseful scene, Winters wins 800,000 francs at a French casino and breaks the bank. The female dealer stabs herself after Winters' winning streak and sprinkles her blood on the money. Winters feels so guilty about her death that he promptly loses the money he had won. He is then talked into becoming a pirate, but on the sea his better nature asserts itself, and he locks the buccaneers under decks and surrenders the ship to the United States Navy. As his reward, he gets to marry his beloved Grace Ellingwood.

Love is a characteristic Ingraham plot ingredient. *The Ringdove* (1846), set near New Orleans, tells the tale of Louis Dumont's love for Isabel Rosal, a love that is hampered by Robert Rosal's hate. But the hero and heroine eventually marry when Robert marries Louis' long lost sister. This sister, Benita, has been brought up by a kindly old smuggler who had treated her with "the tenderness of a cherished house plant" (30), a comparison that ranks highest in the list of strained similes to be found in the Professor's novels.

Most of Ingraham's sea novels begin in Boston, New York, or on

Five Years and Eighty Novels 77

the coast of Maine. The greatest number begin in Boston where most of the Professor's books were now being published. Novels such as *Steel Belt* (1844), which begins in Boston, *The Lady of the Gulf* (1846), which begins in New York, and *The Corsair of Casco Bay* (1844), which is set in Portland's bay, display a familiarity with their settings that must have been gratifying to natives of the various regions. Such knowledge might also have helped sell books. Ingraham's sea novels mark no advance over his early pirate tales, *Lafitte* and *Captain Kyd*. These briefer novels suffer from overused plots and little character development. Some of them have good action scenes which develop genuine suspense, but the majority suffer from the faults already mentioned, faults and characteristics that would appear again.

II *The City and the Country*

Another group of novels that heavily employed Ingraham's knowledge of New York and Boston contrasted the pleasures of country life with those in the city or just dwelt on life in the city. Several of these novels, however, only imply that life is quieter in the country. There was certainly a greater variety of action in the city; thus, the Professor frequently used the city settings.

Edward Austin (1842) may be regarded as the prototype of this genre, a genre that contains many of Ingraham's most notable short novels. The opening of the story finds Edward Austin and his friend Roundy Beebe fishing in a New England trout steam. Ralph Waldron, a young man full of "incipient dissipation" (8), joins them and offers Edward a drink of brandy from his hunting flask. Edward does not drink, refuses Ralph's offer, and lectures the young man on drinking. Time passes, and Edward goes to New York to make his way in the world and to be near Anne Laurens, his betrothed. Mr. Laurens asks Edward to drink a glass of wine to celebrate the pair's engagement, and, when urged by Anne, he does so. With that one taste, however, Edward discovers he likes wine and begins to dine often with the Laurens, for Mr. Laurens takes wine with his meals. Roundy, who has come to the city to serve Edward, starts drinking to keep up with his master and soon gets drunk enough to break his leg. Shortly after this incident, Edward, while drunk, is insulted and challenges Douglas Frazier to a duel. Frazier kills Edward; Mr. Laurens realizes his wine marked the beginning of Edward's fall and dies of his guilty feelings. Anne goes insane and dies in an asylum. Though Roundy's broken leg is amputated, he survives to return to the country sadder but wiser. One of the traps, then, that the city holds for the unwary is liquor. One drink leads to another, and the result is often death.

Another hazard for men is women. *Harry Harefoot* (1845) tells the tale of young Harefoot who comes to Boston to work for a merchant. He soon is drinking, swearing, and breaking the Sabbath after coming under the influence of bad company. To complete his ruin, he is seduced by a fallen woman and eventually dies in a guilty delirium. Richard Berkeley, in *Berkeley* (1846), is redeemed after he falls in the city, but his case is not typical. Most Ingraham male characters are doomed once they commit the first sin.

Austin, Harefoot, and Berkeley illustrate the hazards that await young men in the city while Biddy Woodhull, in *Biddy Woodhull,* displays one of the evils peculiar to young women. Biddy, to escape an unpleasant home situation, leaves her family and, accompanied only by her faithful dog Bruin, comes to New York to find a job. Biddy goes to an employment office that is run by Beal Tucker, a man who plays pimp to Fitz Henry Barton who pays his agent well for securing innocent, buxom young girls. Though Barton is one of the villains of the story, he often comes through as a humorous character. After an evening of drunken revelry he is practically helpless:

"Half past eleven—dem this wine! I feel sick! . . . Frid! Frid, I say!" . . .

"Beg pardon, massa," said the genteel valet. . . .

"I tell you, Frid, you must always be at the door; what can I do alone by myself, when I wake up? It's dem unhandsome, in you, Frid!" . . .

"Where's my gin-cock-tail? Don't you know I am good for nothing— just like a dem rag in the mornin', 'till I get my gin-cock-tail?" (22-23)

Fortified by his gin cocktail, Barton soon makes an attempt on Biddy's chastity, but Bruin grabs the profligate youth by the neck and saves his mistress. Biddy marries Edward Morris after she attends school for two years to make herself worthy of him.

Biddy retains her virtue and is rewarded, but the fallen women in Ingraham's novels are always punished. Their sin is sexual intercourse, and, once committed, death is inevitable. *Eleanor*

Sherwood (1844) is a case in point. Eleanor seduces black-haired Walter Blake, and both give themselves up to passion. Both are soon arrested on a forgery charge, but Eleanor is freed. She goes to visit Walter in prison and, in a scene that owes much to the "Kentucky Tragedy," gives Walter a knife. Both stab themselves and die. The Kentucky Tragedy, an actual event in American history, was explored two years prior to Ingraham's novel by William Gilmore Simms in his *Beauchampe: or, the Kentucky Tragedy* (1842). Simms's account of the lovers who attempted to kill themselves in jail may have influenced the ending of *Eleanor Sherwood*, but the ending is the only major part of the Tragedy Ingraham used.

La Bonita Cigarera; or the Beautiful Cigar Vender (1844) and its 1844 sequel *Herman DeRuyter* capitalized on the interest still felt in the 1841 murder of the beautiful Mary Rogers, the most famous cigar vendor in New York. Edgar Allan Poe's "The Mystery of Marie Roget" (1842) is based on the same tragedy, but the authors reached different conclusions about the murder. Ingraham suggests that the girl was not murdered at all, that she was discovered to be the daughter of an English nobleman, and that she was rescued from her lowly position and returned to England in secrecy so that her lowly occupation would not embarrass her wealthy relatives. Poe is more faithful to the actual case; in his tale, Marie is murdered, but her murderer is not specifically named although he is apprehended. Ingraham's version is full of digressions and not as tightly organized as Poe's tale, but Ingraham's has more action and a species of narrative power that holds the reader's attention more securely than does Poe's more cerebral account.

Ingraham used another actual event as the basis for a novel on the subject of fallen women. *Frank Rivers* (1843) is based on the 1836 Helen Jewett murder in Boston.[3] Hart Granger, the protagonist, is a student at a Northern university. He discovers Ellen Emery on an outing, takes her to his college room, and seduces her. Going to New York with his new mistress, Hart soon tires of Ellen and abandons her. It is not long before Frank Rivers falls in love with Ellen and is seduced by her. Rivers leaves the country on business and, while he is gone, Ellen drifts from one man to another before finally joining the staff of a "fashionable brothel" (28). Her career is halted while she gives birth to Hart's child, but she soon resumes her profession and takes up again with Frank, who has returned to New York. Ellen sees that Hart, who is now studying to be a minister, is going to wed the governor's daughter and writes him not to marry since he is a father. Hart comes to see Ellen and buries a hatchet in the girl's head. He flees to France, totally escaping punishment. Frank is arrested for the murder, and, although he is eventually freed, he becomes an exile from America.

Frank Rivers is a memorable tale and a powerful one. That the murderer went free is an unusual twist that occurs in few Ingraham novels. Most reviewers did not survey the Professor's shorter novels, but the critic for the *Mississippi Free Trader* did not ignore *Frank Rivers*. The reviewer blasted the tale as not being "pure" and criticized Ingraham for employing his pen to write such a novel.[4] Ingraham had told his readers that the purpose of the story was to show the steps that led to ruin in hopes that other people would keep out of the same type of trouble. But the moral, confined to the last paragraph, reads exactly as the afterthought it probably was.

Actually, many of Ingraham's shorter novels have didactic conclusions, but few are convincing. One tale of city life that is more natural in its implied moral is *Paul Deverell* (1845). As the story opens, Paul has just been released from a three-year prison term. His fortunes as he tries to begin life again are well-narrated. He has trouble getting a job because he has been in prison and is fired from one job after his employer learns about his past. Through an act of heroism he is offered a job, but he has to be proclaimed innocent of his offense before many people will have anything to do with him. A reader of this tale might well be convinced that it pays to stay out of the way of the law.

These short novels of the city are generally impressive, and their points are clear: a man or woman has a better chance to remain moral, out of trouble, and lead a happy life if he or she stays away from urban areas. If one ventures into the city, he will need all the strength he has to resist temptation; once tempted and fallen, an individual often ends up dead or in the gutter. Individuals can be penniless and survive in the country; people without money in the city, however, have a difficult time simply staying alive and frequently turn to crime and immorality. Ingraham capitalized on these ideas and probably confirmed the thoughts of many about the city as a place of evil, but he was not a social reformer and was apparently not interested in promoting change. His main concern was to make his stories suspenseful and graphically realistic—a realism, incidentally, that was well ahead of its time. He had not used these city-country plots before *Edward Austin,* and he may be regarded as an American pioneer in the genre. Though he overemployed the basic situations once he discovered them, his modest achievement should not be ignored.

III Novels With a Purpose

Few of Ingraham's novels are explicitly moralistic: this didacticism seems often to have been added as an afterthought. A very few tales from beginning to end remind the reader that the writer has a moral purpose and is sticking to it. Two of these stories may represent the group.

Charles Blackford was written to illuminate the "false estimate between professions and trades" (3). Ingraham indicates that "We have written full enough about pirates, romantic Castilian maidens, and bearded and becloaked Spanish Dons, and mean, hereafter, in some degree to atone for these sanguinary perpetuations by devoting our pen, so long as we can handle one, to encounter and put to shame this most heartfelt of all errors" (3). Charles is a twenty-two year old Yale senior who is a beneficiary, a charity student, at the college. Since Charles' father, a poor minister, believed that his son should work with his head, certainly not with his hands, he sent his son to Yale. But he sent him with no money, so Charles has been teaching between sessions in order that he may continue at the college. The novel begins on the last day of the term when Charles has some accounts to settle and no money with which to pay them. He is able, however, to borrow what he needs to meet his obligations.

Charles graduates, goes home, and saves Grace Gordon after a boating accident. Charles likes Grace, but she is socially his superior because she has money. He tries to forget her. Though a graduate of Yale, Charles' general education has not prepared him for a profession; accordingly, he turns to law and is licensed after three years of study. He goes to Boston to practice but cannot pay his bills and is thrown into jail. After a gentleman pays his debt, Charles begins to make money; he marries Grace and goes on to become rich and a Representative to Congress. This tale, full of the moral for which it was written—that no one should look down on another who works with his hands or who has no money—does have a happy ending. A less pleasant ending might have further dramatized the point, but Ingraham seemed to feel that Charles had suffered enough because of his father's insistence that Charles enter a profession.

Mate Burke (1846) is an interesting exercise in environmental sociology. Twin English-born boys are separated one night in Boston. Dick Cone is raised in a tavern by thieves; the other boy, Edgar Gray, is raised by well-to-do people. Dick, who eventually becomes a thief himself, later kills a man and is hanged. Edgar, however, rises to become the attorney general of Massachusetts. Ingraham's point, of course, is that the proper environment is necessary for a person to realize his potential and be an asset to society.

Mate Burke not only shows the effect of environment on two people, but it also, like *Charles Blackford,* shows that wealth helps improve an environment. Money, of course, was something that forever eluded Ingraham. Wealth and material goods are frequent subjects in his novels; Ingraham knew what money could do for a person and seldom let his readers forget it. Consequently, the motif of most of these didactic novels is that financial prosperity is almost indispensable to human well-being.

Ingraham was writing these novels in a well-established tradition. Samuel Richardson's *Pamela* (1740), considered by some to be the first English novel, and William Hill Brown's *The Power of Sympathy* (1789), considered by others to be the first American novel, are both didactic in intent. Other early American novels, like Susanna Rowson's *Charlotte Temple* (1794) or Charles Brockden Brown's *Wieland* (1798), are filled with moralistic advice. In the writings of Ingraham's 1840s contemporaries, there is also much didacticism; most of it appeared in saccharine poetry and prose in such periodicals as *Godey's Lady's Book* and the *Ladies' Companion.* There was, of course, Grace Aguilar's *Home Influence* (1847) and E. D. E. N. Southworth's *Retribution* (1849), but the major burst of didactical writing came in the 1850s with the "damn mob of scribbling women"—whom Hawthorne envied—and continued with several of the famous "Dime Novels," the first of which was published in 1860.

IV The American Dream

The idea that one could attain wealth, and, that, with determination, rise to almost unlimited success is part of American folklore and mythology. Both the history and literature of the United States boast numerous examples of people who achieved success even though their origins were lowly; America itself is an example of how a few small colonies acquired preeminent power. Ingraham wrote several novels that illustrate this "American Dream."

Jemmy Daily (1843) is the tale of a poor eleven-year old in Boston. His father is a drunkard, and Jemmy often has to protect his mother from his father's drunken blows. He invests four pence halfpenny in newspapers and begins selling them. He is a success because he sings as he sells:

> 'A cent will take you to Japan
> To Turkey or the Isle of Man;
> Tell you what the Sultan's doing,
> How in Spain a war is brewing;
> Tell you who is dead, or marries,
> And how the Southern mail miscarries;
> And all things else in shape of news,
> From price of stock to price of shoes:
> So come and for a penny buy
> What rich will make both you and I!' (42)[1]

This unorthodox method of selling papers is so successful that Jemmy has to buy a dog, Fred, to help defend himself against bullies who are jealous of the young boy's success. After selling papers for a year, he becomes a clerk in Mr. Weldon's business. *Grace Weldon*, the 1845 sequel to *Jemmy Daily*, shows Jemmy as a success in his position of head clerk in Mr. Weldon's commercial house. Jemmy loves Grace Weldon, but he is loved by Frederica Kauphen, who assists Mrs. Daily in the millinery shop Jemmy has provided for his mother. Jemmy is soon made a partner by Mr. Weldon and marries Grace; Frederica dies of a broken heart. If Jemmy were not such a perfect human being, the story might attain some small measure of credibility. As it is, he is so insufferable in his preachings to others about God and goodness that the story would be acceptable only to the most indiscriminate reader.

Another tale of a boy who reaches for something above his station is *The Young Genius* (1843), the story of Edward Brackett's slow rise to recognition as a sculptor. Neither *The Young Genius* nor *Jemmy Daily* is a distinguished piece of work, and neither is worth a second reading. Both have trite plots, familiar characters, and predictable outcomes, but they do illustrate in part Ingraham's contribution to the literature about the "American Dream."

Ingraham's novels about individuals who rise from obscurity to success remind one of the writings of Horatio Alger in the second half of the nineteenth century. Alger often wrote tales of poor but honest newsboys who ended up on the road to success. *Ben Bruce: Scenes in the Life of a Bowery Newsboy* (1901) is one of these stories, but there are many others which employ similar characters in almost identical situations. Alger's tales are undeniably more famous and more numerous, but Ingraham's are no worse if no better. One wonders if Alger had read Ingraham, but the idea of the "American Dream," of course, predates both. To these writers, success and honesty, measured in terms of material achievement, were possible for anyone who had the ambition to rise.

V   *Novels Set in Foreign Countries*

Most of the novels set in foreign countries are historical romances and add no new situations to the ones Ingraham had previously employed. One of these tales, *The Clipper-Yacht; or, Moloch the Money-Lender! A Tale of London, and the Thames* (1845), contains the standard attitudes that Ingraham often expressed toward people of the Jewish faith. The men, like Enoch Moloch, are usurious moneylenders who never forget a wrong or an insult. The women, like Rachel Moloch, are beautiful but loyal to their fathers, a trait that generally makes them particularly dangerous to male Protestant characters. *The Clipper Yacht* is the story of Captain Tudor Dauling, who comes into Enoch's clutches through gambling. Enoch advances him money in return for what is left of Dauling's estate. He then talks his daughter into marrying Dauling so that the moneylender can be revenged on Dauling's Jew-hating father who had struck Enoch thirty-seven years earlier. Dauling does marry Rachel, but Enoch is thwarted because Dauling's father likes her. This story is unusual only in that the Jew is thwarted; Jews in other Ingraham tales always get their revenge even though they may die in doing so.

Montezuma; or, the Serf Chief [1845] is the two-volume novel that Ingraham sold to Harper & Brothers in 1841[5] but which they never published. It details the fall of the tyrant Ulyd and the rise of the serf Montezuma to the throne of the Aztecs. Its fantastically complicated plot is marked by too many characters that contribute too much confusion to the story. The short story version of *Montezuma*, which appeared as "A Legend of the Mountain of the Burning Stone" in the *Southern Literary Messenger*, contains the essential plot elements and holds one's attention much better.

A similar tale is *The Slave King* (1846), another two-volume novel. Set in Spain, the story tells how Alfonso and his band of Spaniards retake their conquered country from the Moors. *Estelle* (1844) recounts a similar tale of the natives on a Carribean island who rebel against the ruling Spaniards.

Ingraham displayed sympathy for the underdog, for the person or country enslaved rather than for the people in power. He seemed to connect the struggle of other people to fight off tyranny with the American struggle to fight off Great Britain. He makes the parallel explicit in *Paul Perril* (1847) when a Connecticut carpenter admonishes four young men to watch what they say about the revolution in Montevideo, Uruguay: "'Keep your own tongues in your heads and don't talk politics; for, being Yankees, you will, of course, take the side of the Patriots outside, and if you are overheard you will be arrested'" (I, 77). Similar motifs are found in other Ingraham novels dealing with wars set in foreign countries. These tales of rebellion are usually superficial in scope, are often only pretexts for a love story, and employ situations Ingraham would use to better advantage when writing of war in America.

Apparently readers liked novels set in foreign countries because Ingraham wrote at least a dozen of them. It is also probable that the tales noted here and others such as *Forrestal* (1845), set in Cuba, and *Bonfield* (1846), set in Bermuda, England, and America, satisfied in some degree a taste for travel literature as well as a desire for an interesting story. There was always some description of the countries involved when Ingraham set a tale outside the United States, but since the author apparently did not travel much, if at all, outside America, his details about foreign countries are minimal and seldom give the reader a feeling that the setting is absolutely essential to the plot of the novel. Ingraham spent most of his time on his love plots and subplots which show that lovers in foreign countries behave much as American lovers do. For all of these reasons, this group of novels cannot be rated very highly.

VI Wars and Rebellions in America

Almost a fourth of the eighty novels that Ingraham wrote between 1842 and 1847 deal with the various wars and rebellions that occurred in America from 1689 to 1812. Most of the tales concern the Revolutionary War.

Leisler (1846) records the story of a Roman Catholic revolt against the Dutch Protestants in New Amsterdam in 1689. The revolt is pushed far to the rear of the main love plot. The Dutch characters are well-drawn, but the heroine, Bertha Leisler, is the only Dutch character who is not portly and slow-thinking, the stereotyped traits of Dutch people according to Ingraham.

The Revolutionary War novels begin, in terms of the war's chronology, with *Pierce Fenning* (1846), a tale of Boston in 1769. The British are in Boston to subdue the rebellious Americans and to impress sailors for the British fleet. Most of the tale deals with several men who are trying to avoid being caught and impressed. These men are aboard a ship, captained by Pierce, which tacks and turns through the islands and channels of Boston Bay in its ultimately successful attempt at dodging the British.

The Free Trader (1847) details the effect that import taxes have on the residents of Newport, Rhode Island, while *Mark Manly* (1843) gives the background of another youth who flees successfully from the British to fight later under John Paul Jones. *The Mast-Ship* (1845) tells of the prelude to the bombardment of Falmouth or, as it was later called, Portland, Maine. Ingraham says that *The Mast-Ship* is founded in fact, but the facts deal with the shelling of Portland; the romantic subplot is certainly invention. *The Mast-Ship* is distinguished only by its great number of typographical errors; the worst occurs when the character Betty Ross has her name changed to Isabel halfway through the tale. Ingraham was particularly fond of naming a female "Isabel"; an "Isabel" or "Bel" appears in approximately ten novels.

Neal Nelson [1845] unfolds a narrative of the siege of Boston in 1776. *Fleming Field* (1845) returns to Boston for a tale of the Stamp Act, a story climaxed by the burning of Governor Hutchinson's house and the tarring and feathering of Clevering, a dissolute British officer.

Arthur Denwood (1846) switches to the War of 1812. In this account, Arthur manages to keep a shipload of smuggled goods from the British who have blockaded the Kennebec River in Maine. Arthur is even able to get the supplies to Boston to keep them away from the British and to keep his sweetheart's father, who is behind the smuggling, from being prosecuted as a British sympathizer. *Freemantle* (1845) and its sequel *Norman* (1845) tell the story of the privateer Freemantle who gives up his career at the end of the war. One of Freemantle's officers, however, decides to become a pirate and steals the ship, only to die in a storm.

Ingraham's best tales of the Revolutionary War are the novel *Burton* and a lengthy short story entitled "West Point" (1838), stories written before the period with which we are presently concerned. His brief war novels suffer greatly in comparison with these two more organized and cohesive stories. Ingraham could write such tales reasonably well when he took or had the time, but he did not have the time from 1842 through 1847 to write such tales slowly or carefully, for he was receiving less money—approximately fifty dollars a novel—for more work. It is no wonder that his novels of war and rebellion sound repetitious. Even though the plots often echo each other, it is quite possible that one reason for their popularity was that they helped foster nationalism or pride in America. The heroes either outfight or outwit the oppressors who are often made to appear ridiculous. Such activities and victories almost certainly helped the nation's morale.

VII *Miscegenation*

The Quadroone concerns miscegenation, but it ultimately avoids the issue by eventually freeing the supposed quadroons from the taint of Negro blood. In three other novels Ingraham does not avoid the issue, and they end tragically for those with Negro blood.

Alice May (1845) tells the story of Edward Orr's love for Alice May. He meets her in a Mount Vernon boarding school, and, after a year of courtship, they are betrothed. Alice returns to her home in Louisiana, and Edward is to follow. He receives one letter telling him to come quickly and a later one which tells him not to come at all. He does go, of course, and arrives at Colonel May's plantation in time to see the Colonel shoot himself in the head. Edward finally discovers that Alice has retired to a convent where she has died of a broken heart. He returns to his home to find a third letter from Alice that tells him she had discovered that she was the bastard daughter of her father and the quadroone Desiree. Alice writes: "Horror filled my mind and rendered me almost insensible! For an instant—only an instant, and once, the idea of concealing my birth - - - occurred to me" (28). But Alice loved Edward too much to let him marry a slave, and she went to the convent to die. Alice, like all of Ingraham's quadroones, has a high sense of honor along with her beauty.[6] Her refusal to keep her birth a secret is a typical reaction.

Marie (1845) and its sequel *Bertrand* (1845) tell a similar story. Marie De Heywode runs to a convent when she discovers she is the daughter of a quadroone slave. Her father, a Byronic hero-villain, drowns himself after poisoning Marie's mother. Charles Bertrand, Marie's betrothed, finds his future wife dead in a convent. Bertrand dies a year later because of his loss and is buried next to Marie. Ingraham seems to have disapproved of the system of concubinage as practiced in Louisiana because of the effects on its victims, but he never criticized the practice except by implication. Perhaps such silence was one indication of his love for the South and its customs.

It was obvious to Ingraham's readers that illicit sex nearly always brings ruin to the parties involved as well as to any offspring of such a union. One Ingraham novel, though it is not about miscegenation, is unusual in its narrative of sex within a family group. *Mary Wilbur* (1845) recounts how Deacon Ely Sparry, "a hypocrite of the first water" (5), marries Charlotte Wilbur for her money. When Charlotte dies, Sparry seduces Charlotte's sixteen-year-old sister Mary. Mary becomes pregnant and is sent to the country so that Sparry's standing in the community will not be blemished. Mary gives birth to a son who is taken from her. Several years pass before she marries a farmer. After four years of marriage and two children, she dies of a broken heart; Mary had never told the farmer that she had, previous to her marriage, borne a child, and the guilt, because she loves the farmer, is too much to endure any longer. Deacon Sparry lives on. Ingraham should be complimented on the realistic touch of allowing Sparry to live, for it stands to reason that not all seducers are so psychologically enmeshed in their guilt that they commit suicide. Such a realistic ending may not have found favor with his audience, but it illustrates to twentieth-century readers that Ingraham was occasionally capable of resisting the idea that all tales should have a happy ending.

VIII *The Grotesque*

There are three stories that do not belong to the categories already mentioned but which are worthy of notice, if only as examples of the grotesque. One of these tales, *The Beautiful Unknown* (1844), is particularly memorable because of one villainous hunchbacked character.

Massey Finke and her hunchbacked son Sammis are grave robbers in Philadelphia who frequently commit murder in order to supply doctors with particular types of corpses needed for dissection. As the story opens, Sammis, who is twenty but looks forty and who has the stature of a nine-year-old, has just drowned a child for calling him "Humpy." Sammis and Massey then steal a pretty twelve-year-old girl who had been found in a boat on the sea by Nelson Nickels and his mother, take her to New York, and force her to be a slave to them. The girl, Adelaide, whose background is unknown, endures four years of servitude before Ogden Neville rescues her from the most grotesque scene in all of Ingraham's work. At the time of Neville's intervention, Adelaide is suspended from a ceiling by her arms. Sammis is sitting on her neck pulling out handfuls of hair while Massey is burning her feet. Sammis and Massey are both sent to jail. Sammis escapes and goes after Adelaide. Adelaide maims him with a hatchet and ties him up, but the dwarf suddenly commits suicide by eating through his breast to his heart. *The Beautiful Unknown* can remind one of wicked trolls or other creatures in fairy tales who torture innocent children. Ingraham's tale, however, does not have the pleasant aura one often associates with fairy tales; it is deadly serious and borders on the sadistic.

Another grotesque tale is *Caroline Archer* [1844]. Caroline is a poor seventeen-year-old milliner's apprentice in Philadelphia who supports her widowed mother and two younger brothers. When Caroline cannot pay the rent, her landlady offers to help Caroline sell her body, something Caroline refuses to do. Meanwhile, Emily Wharton has fallen from her horse and knocked out four of her perfect front teeth. A dentist tells her he could extract teeth from another woman and place them "with the nerve still warm in the cavities of your own" mouth (9). The dentist says the best teeth are to be found in Negresses, but Emily refuses to have the teeth of a Negro in her mouth, and so the dentist places an ad in the paper advertising for any woman who wants to sell four perfect front teeth. Caroline reads the ad, goes to the dentist, and has four teeth extracted so that she can pay the rent. One may assume that the moral of this tale is that everyone has his price; most readers that bought *Caroline Archer,* however, would probably have preferred a more pleasant plot to inculcate the lesson.

Scarlet Feather (1845), which represents what may be regarded as an attempt to write a tale of the noble Indian savage in the manner of James Fenimore Cooper, contains an Indian who possesses an almost grotesque sense of smell. During the Revolutionary War, Natanis is the young chief of the Abenaquies, a tribe of Indians in Maine. He is such a great tracker that he can smell the air and determine if it has been exhaled by another person a short time previously! His brother Sabatis, chief of another tribe, the Tarentines, asks for Natanis' help in fighting the American forces under General Benedict Arnold which are camped nearby. Natanis, however, is friendly to the Americans, stops the people who are trying to warn the British of American troop movements, and gets to marry Willewa, daughter of the Nerijewca chief Canassa, thus bringing peace to the Indians of Maine. Natanis is a typical Ingraham hero even though he is an Indian. He has jet black hair, black eyes, a manly carriage, is the soul of honor, and falls in love at first sight. The tale is a wretched imitation of Cooper. Natanis, a stock character, is not well-developed; he spends most of his time in a love intrigue, and his olfactory capabilities are more laughable than admirable.

Because Cooper's Leatherstocking Tales sold well, Ingraham apparently could not resist imitating them. After the first attempt, however, the Professor was perceptive enough to stay out of the elder novelist's forest.

Obviously Ingraham's briefer novels were written to make money. One can claim they also have aesthetic or didactic purposes, but the prime purpose was to allow him to exist while practicing the profession of his choice. The capturing of an immediate audience was of more importance to him than any other consideration. If Ingraham did receive fifty dollars for each of the eighty novels of this period, he was still paid less for them ($4,000) than for the six books he wrote for Harper & Brothers from 1835 through 1841 ($4,100).[7] It is difficult to blame Ingraham for yielding to the pressure of the dollar and writing what would sell; many writers had yielded to such pressures before him, and many have since. Ingraham's shortcomings as an author cannot be denied; the reasons for them, however, can be noted and understood.

One deficiency is that many of Ingraham's shorter novels suffer from a lack of planning. The Professor either did not try to plan or was not capable of planning most of his shorter novels to take place in brief compass. Some padding does occur in a few tales like *Beatrice* (1847) which has each major character repeat, from his viewpoint, the progress of the story. This repetition would not be a negative trait if each character had a different perspective on the action, but that is seldom the case.

It would be impossible to argue that all of the shorter novels have intrinsic merit, but there are several decent tales in Ingraham's massive output from 1842 through 1847. Although there is little to commend in most of them, some do have intriguing plots, well-executed scenes, interesting characters, and flashes of realism. Whether the reader accepts what Ingraham wrote, it remains clear that his novels are a good index to the public taste of the 1840s. Such novels as *The Dancing Feather, Frank Rivers, La Bonita Cigarera,* and *The Midshipman* deserve an audience with those interested in the period, in Ingraham, or in the history of the American novel.

CHAPTER 5

Periodical Productions

INGRAHAM'S periodical writing spanned his writing career, and no study of the man could pretend completeness without a brief overview of the material that he wrote for ephemeral as well as for the better-known publications. The problems of identification and location that confront any student of the Professor's fiction are overwhelmingly multiplied when he considers the over one hundred piece periodical output of the man. There is no complete bibliography of his periodical productions[1] and may never be. Ingraham himself left only one definite reference to an extant periodical story.

Ingraham wrote for newspapers, magazines, and gift books, and to them he contributed essays, letters, fiction, and poetry. Many of the pieces were republished elsewhere, making the task of compiling a complete bibliography nearly impossible, especially since the files of some periodicals he was known to have published in, the Boston *Uncle Sam*, for instance, are no longer extant. Students of nineteenth-century periodical publishing have not been aware of the prolific Professor's contributions. He certainly set no trends, for he wrote the types of things that were readily marketable, but his works do reveal the mind of the writer as well as the reading taste of the nineteenth-century periodical public.

I *Travel*

Ingraham's periodical publishing career began in 1833 and lasted at least until 1858; for a few of these years no contributions can be found, but this fact does not necessarily mean there were none. The Professor began his periodical career with the material that formed his first book—travel observations.

The first number of an anonymous series of "Letters from Louisiana and Mississippi By a Yankee" was published in the *Natchez Courier: and Adams, Jefferson and Franklin Advertiser* on August 23, 1833.[2] Written from a ship at the mouth of the Mississippi River below New Orleans, the letter pictured the author as he was ready to ascend the river. Ten more "Letters," dealing with various aspects of life in New Orleans in the early 1830s, were published by December 20, 1833. Sometime during 1834 the name of the paper was changed to the *Courier and Journal,* but only one issue survives from 1834, that of December 26,[3] and it does not contain one of the "Letters." Judging from *The South-West,* at least twelve "Letters" must have been published in 1834. The problem of the missing letters is another illustration of the difficulty of compiling a complete Ingraham periodical bibliography. Even when there is the strongest possible circumstantial evidence that his work was published, the periodical itself is often not extant.

The other three extant pieces in the series appeared in the *Courier and Journal* in January, 1835. These letters, which became chapters 5 through 7 of volume 2 of *The South-West,* indicate that a possible thirteen later ones were published. The three *Courier and Journal* letters describe various aspects of Natchez, Mississippi; the most interesting is the one that describes "Natchez Under the Hill," the virtually lawless community that sprang up on the Mississippi under the bluff where the city of Natchez proper is located. Though more respectable in 1830 than in previous years, "Natchez Under the Hill" still boasted "dancing houses, bar-rooms, houses of ill-fame and gambling rooms. . . . Here is heard the sound of the violin, the clink, of silver upon the roulette and faro tables, and the language of profanity and lewdness, day after day and night after night, which, so far from being interrupted by the intervention of one day in seven, is augmented so far as to peculiarly distinguish that day, by a closer and more orthodox devotion to their favorite pursuits and amusements."[4] The traveler notes that such activities are certainly found in other cities, but Natchez residents have had the good sense to keep it "from her vitals," away from the main portion of the city.

A second series of travel letters entitled "Correspondence of the Natchez Courier" began to appear in the Natchez *Weekly Courier & Journal* on April 21, 1837. This series, which ran almost weekly for six months, picks up where the "Letters" and *The South-West* left off. It chronicles Ingraham's travels up the Mississippi from Natchez to St. Louis; then the Professor heads south to Cairo and goes east to Louisville on the Ohio River. His ultimate destination is New York. This sequence of letters formed the basis of two series later published in the *Ladies' Companion*. "Dots and Lines, or, Sketches of Scenes and Incidents in the West" (1839) and "Sketches in the West" (1840-1841) are only slightly different from the original.

These letters, with *The South-West,* form a valuable contemporary picture of regions unfamiliar to most Americans in the 1830s. The sketches of the towns and villages visited are well drawn, and equally interesting are several comments on the costs of buying and maintaining the steamers that made these voyages possible. Pilots were paid as much or more than captains, as Samuel Clemens was to discover. If a steamship lasted five years, Ingraham reported, it was then generally considered old and unfit for further use. The Professor's interest in new sights and new information is evident throughout these narratives.

"Extracts from the Journal of a Passenger from Philadelphia to New Orleans" appeared in the *Gentleman's Magazine* in late 1838. The first two segments of his four-part series are fundamentally the same as chapters 4 and 5 of *The South-West;* Ingraham had again sold part of the account of his popular travels under another name, but there are some definite differences.[5] The most interesting new material is a report of the visit to "King Neptune," an event that would also appear in the 1847 novel *Paul Perril.* Though it is readable, the material is padding and an obvious attempt to make his essay sound original. Ingraham states that "It was fortunate for some of our tyros that we were not bound into Havana" for they would have had to cross the Tropic of Cancer to get to it, and Neptune would have to make his customary visit.[6] In the very next paragraph, however, he is in latitude $0°$, which is the equator and where "Neptune" also appears. These figures mean that Ingraham voyaged almost $25°$ south of Cuba instead of passing between Cuba and the Florida Keys as the text indicates. The padding is not as obvious in the last two "Extracts," which reprint much of the material from chapters 6 and 7 of *The South-West* (volume 1) and some from the first two "Letters" of 1833.

Ingraham eventually arrived in New York, for still another

Ladies' Companion series, entitled "Glimpses at Gotham," chronicled the sights of that metropolis in 1839. The undistinguished series is unfinished; the fourth number says the next essay would describe the Bowery; but if it was written, it was never printed in the *Ladies' Companion.*

After all these wanderings it is not surprising that Ingraham would discuss his views about traveling. For a man that moved around the country almost all of his life, the conclusion he reaches, that traveling is definitely *not* pleasurable, is perhaps surprising, but his arguments are effectively and humorously stated.

All travel is attended with hurry, bustle, disappointment and vexation of spirit. There is the baggage to see to, waiters to bawl after, porters to quarrel with, landlords to growl at, cold and rain, vicissitude of season and climate to contend with, there is the fear of boilers bursting, and of stages upsetting—the annoyance of close state rooms, and unchanged sheets—money taking itself wings, and flying from you on all sides.

The Professor concludes with

If I had my own will, I should never place my foot on stage or steamboat more, but in some quiet corner of the world, where the noise of escaping steam, the horn of the stage driver, the sound of a hotel dinner bell, have never penetrated—where, secure in my own quietude, I should regard travellers as a set of desperate men, whom heaven has visited with a desperate madness, and be thankful for my sanity in the midst of such universal lunacy.[7]

Several of the stories that Ingraham contributed to various periodicals were obviously influenced by what the author saw and heard during his travels. One, "The Bivouac" (1842), is the tale of a gentleman who is voyaging south to find and redeem, if he can, his profligate son who has strayed from the paths of virtue. He and a group of other travelers camp at the mouth of the Ohio to wait for a southbound steamer. They are attacked at night by a gang of thieves. The gentleman shoots the leader, discovers it is his son, goes insane, and dies himself. Another tale, "The Spectre Steamer" (1841), tells of a ghost ship manned by skeletons that travels the Mississippi River, and, to the wonder of other travelers, maneuvers on land.

Still another story that grew out of Ingraham's travels is "The

Sacred Fire" (1838). It originates from a description of Indian mounds near Natchez, mounds that the author mentioned in volume 2 of *The South-West*. The narrator sees a small, brilliant, smokeless flame burning over a subterranean passage in a mound, enters, and finds a seven-hundred-year-old man who needs someone to restart the sacred fire. The narrator obliges him, and, in one of the oldest of trick endings, wakes up to discover that he has been dreaming. None of the tales is memorable. The trick ending of "The Sacred Fire" destroys any credibility; the reaction of the gentleman in "The Bivouac" is excessive and barely credible; "The Spectre Steamer" creates good suspense, but lack of characterization destroys the reader's interest in the plot.

At least four stories deal with the guilty passions to be found in New Orleans and its environs. "Carlota, the Nun of San Eliseo," "The Assassin's Sister," and "The Black Patch" do not merit extended consideration because they all illustrate a similar theme—that New Orleans' passionate natives will stop at nothing to get their way. "The Quadroon [*sic*] of Orleans," however, appeared two years before *The Quadroone* (1841) and should be noted as a precursor of it. Baron Eugenie Championet loves Emilie at first sight but discovers that she is a quadroone and knows, therefore, that he cannot marry her. He does make her his mistress, gets her pregnant, settles a good income on her, and leaves her. Eighteen years later, Championet's legitimate son almost marries his father's illegitimate quadroone daughter. Emilie falls dead; her daughter dies of a broken heart, and Championet and his son are soon killed in battle. None of these New Orleans stories is very pleasant despite the fact that they are reasonably well-written and cohesive. Ingraham's descriptions of New Orleans in *The South-West* and in the "Letters from Louisiana and Mississippi" are the most pleasant pictures he painted of the city.

II *Humor*

Humor is not foreign to Ingraham's writings, but humorous passages are usually short, and the Professor wisely attempted few humorous stories. Those he did write usually exhibit too much straining for too few laughs. Some of his serious stories are often funnier than the ones he tried to make humorous. One story that attempts to be amusing and succeeds is "Mrs. Nicholas Muggs" (1839), one of the four tales Ingraham contributed to the gift books of his era. Mrs. Angelina Celeste Higgins Muggs, the wife of a prominent merchant in a New England seaport, wants desperately to be admitted into the highest social class of the town. She gives a party and invites all the proper prominent people. She decides that "Muggs" looks horrible written on her invitations and decides to claim "Muggs" is a corruption of "Marquis" so as to have an aristocratic name. But even an aristocratic name does not entice the elite to her party. Soon, Mrs. Mannering, a lady that shunned Mrs. Muggs' party, decides to have one herself, and the Muggs do not get an invitation. The angry Mrs. Muggs sends notes to all those who received invitations saying the scheduled party would take place one week earlier than previously noted. Mrs. Mannering discovers the hoax in time and sends out postponements. Mrs. Muggs sends out another set of date changes. When the party does finally take place, Mrs. Muggs attends in disguise and is caught. As a result, Muggs divorces his social-climbing wife. Summaries seldom capture the true flavor of a piece of humorous writing and that, unfortunately, is the case here. Much of the humor in the story comes from the agonized efforts of Mrs. Muggs as she tries to be "respectable."

A story that fails to be humorous is "The Robber in Boots" (1844), a variation of the old narrative of the naive country youth going to visit the big city. The tale is predictable; the youth gets laughed at, is robbed, and returns to the paternal home sadder but wiser. The humor is forced and the story undistinguished. The basic problem with Ingraham's humorous stories is sharply evident here. He labors to be funny and does not succeed. In describing the protagonist the author notes that "He had a father and a mother, as most young gentlemen have had, except those who have been found in Champagne baskets at bachelors' front doors!" (182). He had a voice "like a penny whistle stuck inside of a French horn!" and was "tall, green and delightfully unsophisticated!" (183). The hero had "a Henry Clay lip— Heaven save the mark!" (183) and a mouth that looked like a clam. Exclamation marks do not produce humor any more than Ingraham's asides, and the cumulative effect of such devices is wearying.

III *The Sea and Ships*

For a man who wrote so many novels about the sea, it is quite surprising that only three periodical stories deal with the subject. A reading of two of them, "The General's Niece" (1843) and "The Kennebec Sloop" (1845), reveals a possible reason for the anomaly—both of these stories are little more than anecdotes. "The General's Niece" is the romantic tale of a young lady who is kidnapped from her father's home near Havana so that she may wed the man she loves. "The Kennebec Sloop" tells of an engagement of a Yankee blockade runner with a British ship in the War of 1812. Ingraham performed more ably when he developed his sea stories more fully. His lengthiest periodical sea story, "The Dancing Star: or, The Smuggler of the Chesapeake" (1857), was eventually published as a novel. The narrative details the evil passion of Nevil Beachampe for Alice Beaufort while telling another tale of revenge set in the framework of an account of smuggling activities on the Virginia coast. The story is well told, yet it fails to generate much interest because the characters, even the villains, are too tame, too ordinary, and too predictable. Nevil Beachampe is a colorless Byronic hero-villain; Alice Beaufort is an insipid heroine. Elliot Beaufort and Captain Henry Mainwaring are the mildly heroic heroes. Part of the lack of appeal of this story may be attributed to the fact that it was published almost ten years after the Professor's last sea novel. He had used all the characters and almost all of the situations before and to better effect.

IV *Biography and Criticism*

One of the most prestigious periodicals to which Ingraham contributed was the *Southern Literary Messenger*. The *Messenger* published two tales and a four-part series of "Biographical Sketches of Living American Poets and Novelists" in 1838. The "Biographical Sketches" were originally published in the Natchez *Weekly Courier & Journal* in 1837, but Ingraham did make some few changes in his sketches before they were published in the *Messenger*. These "Biographical Sketches" are interesting for what they reveal of Ingraham's perceptions of other writers and indicate to some degree his idea of what good literature is.

The essay on Francis William Thomas displays a knowledge of eighteenth-century English literature as well as a reverence for "The transcendent genius of Scott." Ingraham himself, as has been noted, derived much from the novels of Scott. Here the Professor goes on to note what would become a tenet of much of his writing: "Perhaps it may be laid down as an undeniable proposition, that no novel can *live*, unless it is based on some remarkable historical event, which, like leaven in the lump, leavens the whole, infusing into it a principle of perpetuity. Independent of the genius of the author, this is the great secret of the Waverley novels."[8]

Another sketch, that of James Fenimore Cooper, showed a knowledge of the rise of the American novel from Jeremy Belknap to 1838. Ingraham thought Cooper was the most distinguished American novelist. "The forest, ocean, and camp, constitute the legitimate empire of Mr. Cooper's genius," he wrote. Cooper

had explored the empire of American fiction, before untrodden, and proved to the world that Europe was not alone the land of story. He had shown that ivied walls, time-worn castles and gloomy dungeons, were not necessary to make a land a land of romance; that the war of the revolution rivalled, in romantic interest, the wars of the crusades; that the Indian warrior equally with the turbaned Saracen, was the theme of the romancer; and that heroes need not always to be clad in iron-mail, nor heroines have only knightly lovers sighing at their feet, or breaking lances and heads to attest to their devotion.[9]

Ingraham set most of his novels in America and made maximum use of the Revolutionary War. He, like Cooper, believed in the resources of America for novelists.

In the fourth essay of the series, one on William Gilmore Simms, the "most prominent novelist in the south," Ingraham repeated his belief that "The American novelist, if he would be deserving of the name, should weave his tales alone out of the fertile legends of the New World."[10] The critic objected to Simms' *The Fall of the Goth* on the grounds that it did not have an American setting; he thought most of the novels with Southern settings, particularly *Mellichampe*. Ingraham's series was, as he says, aimed at introducing a writer's work and was not intended to be overly critical. The series, then, must be judged acceptable. It contains no startling pronouncements, but it does indicate that its well-read author had a wide acquaintance with different types of American and English literature and that his judgments had some firm bases.

V Chivalry

Though Ingraham preferred American settings for the works of American writers, he strayed from America on several occasions. He wrote one series of stories set in the age of chivalry. Four "Tales of the Knights of Seven Lands" appeared in five installments in the *Boston Miscellany* in late 1842 and early 1843. The series employs the old device of travelers (in this case, knights) who decide to rotate stories to pass the time. A Spanish knight tells how young Alarcos won his knight's spurs. The second storyteller, the French knight, tells how Alarcos ignored his betrothed wife and married another. A problem arises since the betrothed is the daughter of the king. The king tells Alarcos to murder his wife; Alarcos does. The German knight tells the third tale, and the fourth, that of the Venetian knight, is unfinished because the periodical ceased publication before the story and series were completed. These four tales, with the addition of two others, were published in 1845 as *The Knights of Seven Lands*. The volume contains only six tales, not the promised seven. Ingraham miscounted, for the award for the best story, the palm of knightly honor, is given at the conclusion of the sixth tale. One other story of chivalry, "The 'Black Knight's Ride' " (1840), which appeared in *Godey's Lady's Book*, is as full of valor, heroics, and blood as the others. That Ingraham, as romantically inclined as he was, wrote such tales is not surprising, but they are not as effective as his more contemporary romances. Obviously, the author strained too much to achieve the results he wished, for the tales contain stilted language and are too serious to win much favor with readers who thought that chivalry involved more lightness, more tales of fair ladies, and less bloodshed.

VI Attempts at Poetry

Another area in which Ingraham was less than signally successful was poetry. He wrote at least eight poems for periodicals, and, following the practice of Sir Walter Scott, he penned several lines of poetry for a few of his novels. Only one of the periodical pieces bears much scrutiny.

"Lines to the Bunker-Hill Monument" is perhaps Ingraham's best poem:

> There stand, fair column of enduring rock,—
> Thy brow in heaven, thy foot upon the height
>   Which erst did reel beneath the fearful shock
> Of charging squadrons and the rushing fight!
>   Temple of freemen, lift thy head on high!
> Beacon for the oppress'd in every clime;
>   Eternal soar towards the arching sky,
> Braving the lightnings and the shafts of time!
>   And, long as thou in pillared pride shall stand,
> May Peace and Art beneath thy shadow rest;
>   May war, that *made thee,* cease in ev'ry land,
> And all the borders of our shores be blest!
>   And, long as men, in awe, shall gaze on thee,
> May thy stern finger silent tell the story
>   That where thou standest, there did Liberty
> Seal, in her blood, Columbia's deathless glory.[11]

This sixteen-line poem, consisting of four quatrains, was written to commemorate the erection of the Bunker Hill monument at Boston. The monument was completed in 1843, very shortly after Ingraham printed his poem, and commemorated the June 17, 1775, Revolutionary War battle that was fought there. Lines two through four indicate deft use of run-on lines. The monument is personified as a "Temple" and as a "Beacon"; the author hopes for a cessation of war for as long as the monument stands "in pillared pride."

Other Ingraham poems are largely derivative. "The Raritan" is an 1841 effusion addressed to the Raritan River in New Jersey. The poem employs the concept of mutability by noting how time has changed the speaker but not the eternal river. While "The Raritan" reminds one of Wordsworth in its expressed love for the river, "The Old Mansion" (1842) sounds as if the author had borrowed some ideas from Oliver Goldsmith's "The Deserted Village." "The Old Mansion" tells the tale of a fine old house where children and families lived, played, and loved; it burned after the last inhabitants died. "Human Life" is also on the theme of mutability; the poem indicates that all people, no matter what their rank, are "to one fate consigned."[12]

Ingraham realized he was not a good poet. He lamented in an 1841 letter to publisher George Roberts that "alas! the Muses have not blessed me!"[13]—and he was right! His inflated diction and derivative subject matter would not have won him many new readers. Ingraham even wrote a story about the bleak future of a poet. "The Poet's Curse; or, 'We Shall Be Rich To-Morrow'" appeared in 1844 in the Professor's most frequent periodical outlet—the *Ladies' Companion.* A penniless poet, Edward Cameron, is searching for a publisher in a cold Boston November. He desperately needs money to buy medicine for his dying wife. Finally he is asked by a wealthy patent pill manufacturer to write a poem praising his pills. Edward is to deliver the poem the next day, but the manufacturer refuses to give the poet any money in advance. Edward is so desperate and his wife so sick that he writes his father for money. His wife dies during the night, and Edward goes mad; he now raves and writes in a madhouse. Several poor poets appear in Ingraham's ficion, and their fates are seldom better than Edward Cameron's.

VII *The Supernatural*

Some of the more interesting tales that Ingraham contributed to the *Ladies' Companion* were stories of weird, unexplained events or ghost stories. The most pleasant of these is "An Evening at Buccleuch Hall; or, The Grenadier's Ghost." Buccleuch Hall was the former headquarters of several British generals during the Revolutionary War. Now, about seventy years later, a retired American colonel lives there and chooses a stormy night to relate his tale of the grenadier's ghost which he had seen three years earlier. The colonel relates how, at the final stroke of midnight, he heard a heavy step descending the hall stairs. Soon the remains of a melancholy British grenadier captain march into the room to refill his rusty camp lantern with oil:

'What would'st thou further, dread spectre from the tombs?' I demanded, my blood curdling in my veins as I did so. With his skeleton finger still extended towards the table, he replied in a deep sepulchral voice,
'Wine.' (170)[14]

After a few glasses of port, the ghost becomes extremely sociable and requests a cigar but is offered a meerschaum pipe instead. He tells the colonel that he will tell him where some buried treasure is located in the mansion, but, before the grenadier can relate his story, the clock strikes one, and the ghost ascends the stairs and becomes the old hall clock. " 'The only difference I could see, was, that I thought the full moon face [of the clock] looked a little more ruddy than usual, as if it had been indulging freely in old port' " (171). This tale of a thirsty ghost is more often amusing than scary and can easily remind one of the quietly humorous tales of Washington Irving.

Another story, and one with more mystery to it, is "The Green Huntsman; or, The Haunted Villa. A Christmas Legend of Louisiana" (1841). The tale opens on Christmas Eve at a festival that is not only a seasonal party but the wedding night of Henride Claviere and his betrothed Ephèse. The night is also Ephèse's birthday. Suddenly a nearby haunted villa begins to burn, but it is not consumed, though a large tongue of green flame keeps leaping into the air. Don Antonio Baradas offers to explain what this mysterious event means. He tells of an evil, ugly, and rich Spaniard, Don Rolando Osormo, who was hunting for a bride that would be both perfectly beautiful and perfectly blind. He kidnaps a beautiful nun he thinks is blind. He soon discovers, however, that she can see. A dwarf with a single green eye appears to Osormo and says he will blind the lady without destroying her beauty; the dwarf's payment for this deed is to be the souls of any children they may have. Osormo agrees; his wife is blinded, and the couple has seven beautiful daughters, each born on a Christmas Eve.

When the first daughter turns eighteen, she has a birthday party on Christmas Eve, a night which is also to be her wedding night. On that night, a tall, dark stranger dressed in green appears, tells Osormo he has come for the daughter, and leaves with her. After he loses five daughters, Osormo comes to America and builds the mansion, now obviously haunted, and there, in spite of everything, he loses his sixth daughter to the dark stranger. Midnight now comes to the group of guests, and Baradas takes Ephèse, the seventh daughter, and rides into the haunted villa. As he rides, he changes into a dwarf. Ingraham promised a sequel to this tale, but one was never published. These stories of unexplained happenings are well developed and cohesive. They tell just enough to keep the reader in suspense, and, though the characters may be regarded as stock, they are interesting.

VIII The Virtues of Morality

Another group of pieces were tales with a decidedly moral slant. The modern reader will have little patience with these tales; the nineteenth-century reader, however, must have enjoyed them because Ingraham wrote several. In "The Lottery Ticket" (1843), avarice and liquor draw Donald Fay to destruction. Donald is a good and industrious farmer, but, on a trip to sell his produce in New York, he is talked into drinking by some of his friends. While drunk, he buys a lottery ticket, something he later realizes is very sinful. His avarice, however, will not allow him to destroy the ticket; he wins five hundred dollars and is led to buy tickets for a steady two years of losing. His wife dies of a broken heart; his child is adopted by others, and Donald is eventually decapitated by a train. Moral: Do not buy lottery tickets or drink liquor.

One of the most preposterous of Ingraham's moral tales is "Harvey Ross," a three-part story about the evils of chewing tobacco. Harvey Ross is an excellent blacksmith near New Rochelle, New York; he has a beautiful wife, Ruth, and five fine children. Harvey is rising in the esteem of everyone, but he has one bad habit: he chews tobacco. Harvey knows he is a sinner, but he cannot quit:

"I confess the use of tobacco is very foolish, very useless, and I think [it] is injurious to the system. I don't see how you can bear to have me come near you [Ruth]! but it is only *endurance,* for no woman of taste and sensibility can like it. It is a vile habit, Ruth."
  "Then why don't you give it up, Harvey; I am sure I should be glad of it; and so would my poor floors."[15]

The "poor floors" continue to be stained because Harvey does not quit. One Sunday morning, however, he makes the horrible discovery that he is out of tobacco. After church he asks a dissipated neighbor, Besley, if he has a quid to spare. Besley does not and has a few discourteous things to say to the highly moral Harvey. On his way home from the services, Harvey picks up a cigar butt and joyously places it in his mouth. But the cigar soon disintegrates, and Harvey is so miserable that he snaps at his wife for the first time in his life. "Like a man parched with thirst, whose visions and thoughts are all of cool fountains, gushing water, his were filled with the subject of his unnatural and guilty craving."[16] To satisfy his desire, Harvey decides to break the Sabbath by going to town and buying a quid at the local tavern. He buys his quid and is talked into taking one drink. Harvey is horror-stricken at his sins and runs from the tavern. He soon falls upon the earth and writhes in mental agony with the consciousness of his fall. His wife Ruth finds him and tells him their eldest son is ill. Harvey gets the doctor, but the boy dies, and Harvey is sure that "this illness had been sent as a judgement upon him,"[17] and curses God for that judgment. Harvey decides to commit suicide but is saved by a minister and prays to God for forgiveness. From that time Harvey becomes a better man, and he no longer chews tobacco. While this tale would certainly not be popular with today's audience, its type was not unknown in Ingraham's time. Even though the tale is not new as a type, the sin—chewing tobacco—is at least somewhat of a novel approach to the idea that man is a sinful creature and that Christ can help. Ingraham was moving by slow degrees back to the thought that he might become a minister, a step he took three years later.

The three installments of Harvey Ross's tale were part of the thirty-five diverse pieces Ingraham contributed to the *Ladies' Companion* between 1839 and 1844, its last year of existence. These thirty-five pieces were printed in fifty-seven issues, making the *Ladies' Companion* his best popular periodical customer. *The Symbol, and Odd Fellow's Magazine,* accepted eleven moral pieces in 1844 and 1845. Of the moral tales that Ingraham wrote, the majority appeared in the *Symbol.* Omitting the travel sketches, only one other periodical published a group of tales so closely related thematically; these were the historical tales contributed to the *United States Magazine.*

The first tale contributed to the *Symbol,* in June, 1844, was signed "J. H. Ingraham." All the ones after that were signed "Bro. J. H. Ingraham," giving rise to the speculation that he had joined the Order of Odd Fellows. That he understood the benevolent principles of the order may be seen through his 1846 novel *The Odd Fellow* as well as from the *Symbol* stories which all deal with the organization.

Since Ingraham's novels for this period (1844-1845) do not reflect an unusual drift toward highly moral tales, it is reasonable to assume that the *Symbol* tales were written to specification. Only one tale, however, is known to have been definitely written to order—"The Young Artist." The story was written to illustrate a painting owned by Philadelphia publisher Edward Carey, and Ingraham intended that it be published in *The Gift*, a literary annual. Ingraham wrote Carey that he was enclosing "the Ms of the Tale written by me, at your request, To illustrate the painting by Mount, which I saw at your residence, when in Philadelphia. . . . It is, you are doubtless aware, one of the most difficult parts of authorship To write to a painting, weaving it into a story of romance; and the chances are ten to one for a failure on his part who attempts it."[18] The tale does not have a stated moral. It is the story of a sixteen-year-old artist who meets with ignorance and prejudice as he begins his career but who perseveres to win fame and the hand of his faithful sweetheart. The story is not a success, for it is full of clichés. Artist Henry Irvine is talented and misunderstood. Davy Dow is his loyal friend, while Mary Elizabeth Odlin is his faithful girl who waits for seven years while Henry is away making a name for himself. The villain of the piece is Dominie Spankie, the aptly named tyrannical schoolmaster who plies his oaken ferule to Henry once too often. The tale did not appear in *The Gift; Godey's Lady's Book* published it in 1840, and it was popular enough to be reprinted with another novel in 1846.

IX *Tales of America's Past*

The most successful group of Ingraham's periodical contributions consists of those stories and legends that have as their basis some event or individual in America's history. These stories owe some of their interest, it is true, to their quasi-historical background, but Ingraham's ability to hold his reader is by no means based solely on the reader's interest in history.

A major group of romances was published in the pages of the *United States Magazine, and Democratic Review*. These tales were published under the general title "Romance of American History" in four issues from February, 1838, to November, 1839. The first of these was "The Charter, An Historical Tale of Connecticut." The story begins in 1668 as Sir Edmund Andros is leading a band of soldiers to Hartford to demand the Connecticut Charter from the residents. Andros plans to get the Charter with the help of Helen Pierpont who is going to steal it for him. But Catharine Wyllys hears the two plotting and switches the Charter for another roll of parchment. With the "Charter" in hand, Andros takes his troops to the town's council hall and demands the Charter he thinks he already has from Governor Robert Treat. Andros is refused, declares himself governor, and produces his "Charter" which proves to be an Indian deed to hunting grounds. Andros' "proud and confident manner changed, not to one of mortification and disappointment, but to one of vindictive rage. He gnashed his teeth; crumpled the parchment in his hand; flung it to the earth and ground it with his heel."[19] Catharine's lover has put the Charter in the base of a hollow oak tree, and Andros never gets it, though he does take over the colony.

The purpose of "The Charter," as Ingraham notes, was "to combine healthy instruction with that entertainment, which all are bound to expect in a work of fiction" (354). The comment might well be taken as an Ingraham credo; the idea of entertaining as well as giving instruction or a moral is found in some degree in all his novels. The instruction is sometimes oblique, a practice that is really preferable to ending a tale with a stated precept as he did occasionally. The characters in "The Charter" are familiar. Andros and Helen are the dark villainous characters, and Catharine is the fair-haired heroine. The same types of characters in a periodical tale are often found in Ingraham's novels, so one of the main differences between his periodical contributions and his novels is simply length and development.

Ingraham's next romance was a tale that was obviously quite popular, for it was reprinted several times during his life, and a version of it was prepared for the stage. "West Point.—A Tale of Treason" appeared in the *Democratic Review* in November and December of 1838. "West Point," the tale of the treachery of Benedict Arnold, was dramatized by Joseph Breck in 1840. It was reprinted in the *Ladies' Companion* in 1842 as "Arnold; or, the British Spy. A Tale of Treachery and Treason" and printed separately in 1844 and 1847.

The story begins as Arnold prepares to meet Major John André who has come to make the final negotiations with him before allowing the British to take the American fort at West Point. For him Arnold reviews his reasons for turning traitor:

> "I can read the meaning of your glance, Major André," said Arnold, slightly coloring, "and appreciate your estimation of me in relation to the part I am about to act. . . . I am prepared to meet the scorn and contempt of gentlemen, so that the personal feelings that I have in this matter are gratified. Major André, I am an injured man! I have repeatedly fought for, and five times shed my blood in defence of, my country, and she has rewarded me, not only with contumely and neglect, but with open insult. . . . When I resolved to repay my country for the wrongs she had loaded me with, it only remained to decide the best means of doing it, so that I could bring about advantage to myself as well as injury to the cause I was about to desert."[20]

Arnold gives André the plans of West Point, discovers that his treachery is about to be uncovered, and escapes. André is captured and hanged as a spy despite the fact that several believe he was simply the victim of circumstances.

"West Point" is one of the few Ingraham tales without a love plot. The story is built around Arnold and André, and the rapid pace seldom flags. Arnold is believable as the traitor, though André is a bit too much the soul of honor. Given a chance to escape from the Americans, he refuses. Breck's dramatization of "West Point" is similarly well done; it is one of the two surviving dramas based on an Ingraham tale. Breck's contribution was minimal as he himself acknowledged in an introductory note to the drama: "The dramatist of 'West Point' claims but little originality in this composition. His chief merit consists in adapting a well written tale to dramatic representation."[21] Except for the stage directions and the prologue and epilogue in couplets, Breck followed Ingraham so closely that he lifted verbatim most of the speeches in the novel.

One final tale based on American history was also popular. "The Bold Insurgent. A Tale of the Year 1675" is an 1842 story of the rebellion of Colonel Nathaniel Bacon in Virginia and was published in the *Ladies' Companion*.[22] Bacon tried to get a commission from Sir William Berkeley, governor of the colony, to lead men against the Indians who were pillaging the frontier. Berkeley, however, was engaged in profitable trading with the Indians and refused the request. Bacon marched against the Indians anyway and was declared a traitor for his actions.

Berkeley saw that the young cavalier was popular and tried to disguise his hatred of the Virginian by promising him the commission he wanted while secretly issuing an order for his arrest. Bacon saw through Berkeley's plot, burned the capital city of Jamestown, and died soon after "from the effects of poison rubbed upon his saddle by the Indian Cineca" (227)—a unique method of murder.

This tale is primarily interesting as an exciting account of an historical event. One historian of the Rebellion has pointed out that Ingraham drew from several sources for his treatment of Bacon, that Ingraham did not always give credit to his sources, and that he departed from them when it suited his dramatic purposes. Several writers have compared the Rebellion to the Revolutionary War, but, the critic claims, Ingraham does not.[23] Ingraham does indeed draw the parallel, but he does not develop it. He writes, "It is a coincidence worthy of remark, that this rebellion in Virginia took place precisely one hundred years before that of the thirteen colonies" (227). Had Ingraham developed the parallel, his story might be more interesting, but, for him, "the real quintessence of the uprising lay in its dramatization of the spirit of the Virginia Cavaliers,"[24] of the spirit of the noble and honorable men who were among the first settlers of Virginia.

X *The Minister as Writer*

The longest and most developed periodical tale that Ingraham wrote was a product of his years as a minister. *The Evergreen,* an Episcopal publication, ran "Letters from Adina" from August, 1850, through December, 1853. The "Letters" were published in 1855 as *The Prince of the House of David,* Ingraham's best seller and most famous work, a novel to be discussed in chapter 6. The work, first published as a serial, set the stage for another work to appear, a device Ingraham had used before. A postscript to the "Letters" indicated that the

> Roman Centurion, Aemilius [whom Adina married], . . . became Procurator of the Island of Britain in the West, and with Adina, . . . was the first to entertain the Christian Apostle, Saul of Tarsus, otherwise Paulus. . . .
>
> The first establishment of the Faith of Jesus, in this remote Roman

barbaric Province by the Jewish Apostle, and its spread throughout the Island, are to be found written in detail in certain letters, which the daughter of Aemilius and of Adina, wrote to her brother, a Roman knight at Rome.[25]

These advertised letters began to appear in January, 1856, in the *Churchman's Monthly Magazine,* another Episcopal periodical with a limited circulation. This series, entitled "Elfrida, the Druid's Daughter; or, The Cross Planted in Britain. A Tale of the First Century," ran for ten months.

"Elfrida" begins with descriptions of a forest, a castle, and a maiden written with Ingraham's customary descriptive length. Twenty-nine years after Christ's crucifixion, Aemilius, Adina, and their daughter Elfrida Virginia Tullia arrive in Britain; Aemilius is to be the new Roman procurator. After several installments of well-written straightforward narrative to set the basic situation (which involves stopping the Druids from sacrificing humans, keeping peace among the warring tribes, and generally establishing the Christian faith in Britain), Elfrida begins her series of letters to her brother Horatius. Ingraham's skills as a writer are displayed as he details Elfrida's trip to Britain, but when Elfrida notes that Paul has come to Britain, she becomes too involved in giving his history, and the story goes downhill from this point. In fact, the last installment ends so hurriedly that either the publisher decided he did not want three and a half years of story like "Adina," or Ingraham simply decided to end the tale with an eye toward future ventures. The first assumption is probably nearer the truth, since Ingraham returned to the story four years later. At any rate, Elfrida records that Paul has converted many in a miraculously brief time, and the various threads of the story, so carefully begun, are disposed of in paragraphs.

Ingraham used materials from his ministerial work at Nashville as a basis for "Secrets of the Cells" (1855), and from his first parish assignment in Mississippi came the basis of a story entitled "The Midnight Guest" (1855), a tale of a young man who steals the silver from St. Mark's African Chapel near Okolona. Ingraham himself delivers a check for one thousand dollars to get the plate back, and he assures his reader that the thief doubtless came to a bad end, "for unparalleled wickedness, such as his, soon comes to the end of its tether" (343).

Ingraham's next charge at Mobile provided the impetus for several more stories. "Mysteries in My Parish" (1854) is a three-installment tale that tells of a quadroone who has a white infant and abandons her so that she may grow up without the stigma of her mother's race. Another tale published under this general title tells of the misery of a discarded wife of a nobleman. "Sketches from the Notebook of a Parish Clergyman" (1855) relates how the minister was successful in saving a soul. No other autobiographical tales bearing Ingraham's name have been located.

Besides writing tales based on his religious studies and experiences, Ingraham produced a wide variety of contributions on other subjects for many periodicals. He penned accounts based on American history as well as moral tales, supernatural stories, chivalric narratives, pieces of literary criticism, yarns of the sea, brief humorous anecdotes, and travel sketches. Some contributions, like an historical survey of walking canes or an essay on the will, do not fall into particular categories.

Ingraham undoubtedly published other material in periodicals not mentioned here. At the end of *La Bonita Cigarera* is a note that says the novel and its sequel *Herman DeRuyter* were published in the *Yankee*. He is probably referring to the New York *Weekly Yankee*, copies of which are no longer extant for this period.[26] Several other periodical pieces were later printed separately as short novels ("West Point," "The Young Artist," "The Bold Insurgent"), and there were surely others.

It is unlikely that a definitive listing of Ingraham's publications will ever be compiled. All the sources are not known; many items were published anonymously; and some of the known ones no longer exist, but such a listing would not add greatly to Ingraham's stature. The basic types of his contributions have been mentioned, and the reader will doubtlessly realize that—in this instance—more work will reap no benefits. The law of diminishing returns sets in after one has done much reading in Ingraham's short pieces; the more one reads the more one is convinced that the effort is largely wasted. Ingraham's sins as a periodical writer are many. He padded some works and used inflated diction in others. He seldom delivered a complete characterization and often left the impression that his plots could have been better developed. He wrote many moral tales, some of which employed stock characters who behaved in predictable ways. It is easy to understand why Ingraham wrote these tales—he needed the money—but that reason does not soften our estimation of their literary merit.

Ingraham's periodical pieces shared the limelight with the writing of many other contemporary magazine authors. The quality of his work fares favorably when compared with other popular writers such as Lydia Sigourney, Seba Smith, Catharine Maria Sedgwick, Anna Cora Mowatt, and Nathaniel P. Willis, to mention only a few. All mirror the period; all are historically valuable, and all are currently almost ignored. There are some Ingraham pieces, nevertheless, that are sufficiently entertaining to deserve a second look. "The Quadroon of Orleans," "Mrs. Nicholas Muggs," "An Evening at Buccleuch Hall," and "West Point" are readable pieces that display Ingraham's periodical work at his best and might well find readers again if they were reprinted.

CHAPTER 6

The Minister's Literary Products

WRITING was in Ingraham's blood, and his 1847 confirmation into the Protestant Episcopal Church did not eradicate the impetus to authorship, though it did eventually redirect some of his output into different areas. Several works appeared under his name from 1847 to 1855 when *The Prince of the House of David* was published, but they are almost totally forgettable. As noted earlier, *Prince* was written and serialized before its publication in October, 1855,[1] by Pudney & Russell of New York. The novel, however, appearing as it did in an obscure church periodical, was virtually unknown until this book publication.

Ingraham's literary star burned brightest with *Prince's* appearance. The book sold so well and was such a success that the author revised it in 1859. The story was a pioneer achievement in biblical fiction. The Reverend William Ware's efforts in this field, notably his *Julian* (1841), were among the first to transform biblical material into fiction, but Ingraham's three biblical novels sold better, were more popular, and were more influential. They almost certainly helped to pave the way for such later successes as Lew Wallace's *Ben-Hur* (1880) and Charles Sheldon's *In His Steps* (1896). When the definitive history of biblical fiction in America is finally written, Ingraham will deserve a place of prominence.

Ingraham explained his purposes in writing *Prince* in his 1855 introduction. If this work "may be the means of convincing one son or daughter of Abraham to accept Jesus as Messias, or convince the infidel Gentile that He is the very Son of the Lord and Savior of the world, he [the author] will have received his reward for the midnight hours, stolen from parochial labors, which he has devoted to this work" (v-vi). Ingraham also says that "Jesus was *man,* as well as God! In this book He is seen, conversed with, eaten with, as a man!" (vi). Adina, the Jewish maiden who "writes" the thirty-nine letters that comprise

Prince, emphasizes Jesus' humanity primarily through His personal suffering.

Prince begins shortly before Jesus' baptism in the Jordan River and ends forty days after his resurrection. The seventeen-year-old Adina is sent to Jerusalem by her father, Manasseh Benjamin Ben Israel, to be educated in the laws of Moses in the home of her relative Rabbi Amos. The first of her letters to her father, which detail her journey from her home in Alexandria, is almost a guided tour through various places mentioned in the New Testament. She sees Gaza, Mount Moriah, Gethsemane, Mount Olivet, and other sights. She also sees several malefactors crucified on Calvary. At the end of her first letter she casually mentions that there is a new prophet near Jordan.

The new prophet is mentioned again in letter 2. John, a cousin who is betrothed to Adina's cousin Mary, has heard the prophet by letter 3. This third letter also marks the beginning of the subplot of the tale when Adina is rescued from two drunken Roman soldiers by Aemilius, a Roman centurion, who is described as being "as courteous a person as I had ever met with among my own countrymen" (26). Aemilius, of course, is also handsome.

Adina goes to see and hear the prophet John of Jordan, also called John the Baptizer. He dwells alone in the wilderness, coming to the people only to preach and baptize them. He publicly proclaims himself the forerunner of the Messiah, and, by her seventh letter, Adina is able to write "My trembling fingers scarcely hold the light reed with which I am about to write you concerning the extraordinary things I have seen and heard; but they tremble only with *joy.* Oh, my father, my dear, dear father, Messias HAS COME! I have seen him!" (80). But Adina also says that she is anticipating her story and will slow down to tell her father how she made this discovery. This narrative ploy not only allows Adina time to detail her first sight of Jesus, but it also builds some suspense. In telling his story Ingraham, whose ability to create anticipation and interest by hints and direct statements had been well honed by this time, uses his skill to its fullest advantage.

Adina, her cousins Mary and John, and Rabbi Amos go to Jordan to hear John the Baptizer talk about the Messiah before ten thousand people. Like other Jews, Adina expects to hear of a god who will set up an earthly throne and rule. But she learns from her cousin John, who has already talked with the Baptizer, that the Messiah is to be a man of sorrows and one acquainted with grief, that he will be rejected by the Jewish people, that he will be despised for his lowliness and obscurity, and that he will die in ignominy—just as the prophet Isaiah had said.

Adina first sees Jesus on this trip when He comes to be baptized by John in the Jordan. Jesus, she tells us, has "an indescribable dignity and grace of aspect, combined with an air of benevolence and peace that at once attracted me" (109). John the Baptizer knows Jesus at once, tells the assembly who He is, and baptizes Him. After the baptism, light comes from heaven; a dove of fire overshadows Jesus, and the voice of God rings out: "*'THIS IS MY BELOVED SON IN WHOM I AM WELL PLEASED. HEAR YE HIM'*" (112). The multitude is astonished; many fall on their faces in fear; Adina believes she has seen the Son of God.

Adina's father, however, does not believe in this new messiah or prophet, and many of her following letters relate her efforts to convince him. Since the Old Testament prophets said the Messiah would work miracles, miracles appear to be absolutely necessary before Adina's father and other Jews believe in Jesus. Miracles are what Jesus performs through most of the middle section of the novel.

That Jesus has the ability to work miracles with God's help is one of the two major motifs in Ingraham's story. Ingraham appears to be saying that like the Jews in Jesus' day, the mid-1850s public would be most convinced by miracles. The changing of the water to wine during a wedding in Cana is the first miracle noted. Christ feeds ten thousand people with five loaves and two small fish, returns sanity to a maniac named Benjamin, restores life to Samuel and Lazarus, heals the sick with a look, a touch, or a command—all of which Adina carefully records. She also writes that Aemilius is becoming more interested in Judaism, and, by the twenty-second letter, is converted to Adina's faith and receives a Jewish name, Eleazer. She writes her father that "there stands now . . . no further bar to our union" (240).

The other major characteristics of Christ that Ingraham emphasizes are His pain and sorrow. As noted in his introduction, Ingraham wishes to present Christ as man as well as God, for He certainly was both. That He would resist temptation even though

He suffered the same pain as any man is indeed God-like. The cousin John witnesses some of Jesus' agony in His desert battle with Satan. Jesus tells His disciples "'Through suffering only can I draw all men after me!'" (176). Cousin John becomes a disciple and comments that "'Detraction and envy, malice and unbelief, follow [Jesus'] footsteps, and daily his life is menaced, and no place is a place of shelter for his aching head'" (202). Being hated and repulsed by the high priests of the temple in Jerusalem, however, were certainly Jesus' worst burdens, particularly since those priests of God led the wave of disbelief. After one of many rebuffs from those priests who envy too much to believe, Adina hears Him praying to His Father: "At times I could hear him praying and supplicating, in tones of the most heart-breaking pathos; at others, the silence of his room was only broken, at intervals, by sighs and pitiful groans, that seemed to come from a breaking and crushed heart!" (306-7). Adina learns much of Jesus' sorrow and sees many of His miracles, since Jesus often stays with Rabbi Amos when He is in Jerusalem.

The plot begins to move faster when Adina reports, in letter 29, that "Jesus, the Prophet of God, is a prisoner to the Roman power!" (312). Then she tells the background of Jesus' being captured by quoting the disciple John's account of the Last Supper. Jesus told his disciples to love one another, explained how they would react to his capture, and is soon betrayed by Judas Iscariot. Adina is shocked at Jesus' capture, but she does not lose faith in Him because "I have seen him bring Lazarus from the grave, and I will not believe but that He can save himself, and will save himself, from their hands. It is only when I shall behold him really no more—see him really *dead*, that my faith in his divine mission will waver" (326-27). With this statement of less than total belief Adina ends her long twenty-ninth letter.

Letter 30 brings yet another change of tone:

I know not how to write—I know not what to say. Dismay and sorrow fill my heart. I feel as if life were a burden too heavy to bear. Disappointment and regrets are all that remain to me. He, in whom I trusted—He, whom thousands in Judah had begun to look upon as the hope of the nation—He, who . . . would have redeemed Israel—Jesus, has been delivered, this morning, by the Roman Procurator, to be condemned to death, *and they have crucified him!* (328)

With mounting gloom Adina recounts Jesus' treatment at the hands of the Jewish priests Annas and Caiaphas. Jesus is saved from injury by Aemilius and a squadron of soldiers, and it is Aemilius who takes Jesus to Pilate. Pilate sends Him to Herod since Jesus is from Galilee which Herod rules, but Herod returns Him, and Pilate finally condemns Jesus because he does not have enough soldiers to control the unruly Jews.

Adina's gloom vanishes abruptly when, in letter 37, she says: *"Jesus is alive!* Jesus has RISEN FROM THE DEAD! Jesus has proved himself to be the Son of God" (423). Adina severely reproaches herself for not believing in Him and sees Jesus ascend into Heaven forty days after His resurrection, His work on earth completed.

Here the novel ends, but, in the fashion of the day, Ingraham adds a postscript about Adina's future. He explains that Adina and Aemilius are married and that Aemilius later became procurator of Britain. Adina and Aemilius are among the first to entertain the apostle Paul when he comes to preach the gospel of Jesus in Britain. This postscript indicates that Ingraham was considering a sequel to *Prince* even as he finished the novel. That sequel was undoubtedly *St. Paul the Roman Citizen,* the novel the author was contemplating at the time of his death in 1860, portions of which he had published in 1856. Before Ingraham turned his full attention to *St. Paul,* however, he completed two novels based on the Old Testament.

The Prince of the House of David seems to be founded primarily on the Gospel according to St. John,[2] but not everything in the novel is found in St. John. Ingraham used chapter 1 of Acts for Christ's Ascension and the Gospels of St. Matthew, St. Mark, and St. Luke to fill in information on Christ's youth and early manhood. Both St. John and St. Mark emphasize the humanity of Jesus while St. Matthew emphasizes His teachings. It appears that Ingraham was influenced least by St. Matthew because *Prince* does not devote much attention to Jesus' parables or sermons. The novel presents Jesus' humanity by showing Him visiting and helping all classes of people, but more emphasis is placed on His physical sufferings. The most curious thing about the novel is that Ingraham does not devote attention to Jesus' teachings—an approach a reader would expect, considering Ingraham's background as a professor and minister. Adina comments after one of Jesus' sermons that it was "a sermon so full of wisdom, of love to man, of love to God, of knowledge of our hearts, of divine and convincing power, that thousands wept; thousands were chained to the spot with awe and delight, and all were moved as if an angel had addressed them" (242). But no specifics about the sermon are given; in fact, Jesus' command to His disciples that they "Love one another!" (315) is the only direct teaching in the novel.

Jesus is physically described by Pontius Pilate as having "'A form divine, and fit for Apollo. . . . The chisel of Praxiteles nor of Phidias ne'er traced the outlines of limbs and neck like these. He is the very incarnation of human symmetry and dignity'" (363). Most of Ingraham's heroes and heroines have similar superior physical characteristics. The dark eyes of Jesus and His triumphs over his enemies are also Ingraham staples, but here the typical characteristics end, and the unique characteristics of Jesus begin. He is a humble individual; even when people wish to thank Him for His many miracles, He shuns their expressions of gratitude. Jesus' sufferings are another evidence of His human qualities. When He prays on Mount Olivet, "his countenance was convulsed with anguish; and upon his brow stood great shining drops of sweat, mingled with blood, which oozed from his pallid temples, and rolling down his marble cheeks, dropped to the ground. Never had we beheld a human visage so marred by sorrow, so deeply graven with the lines of agony" (318-19). He works miracles as an emissary of God but also because the people expect miracles from God's prophet and would not believe in Him otherwise. Adina is a good index to this fact, for she loses faith in Jesus when He allows Himself to be captured by the Jews and does not use His abilities to free Himself or mitigate His sufferings. Jesus meets death with courage and rises after three days to the utter consternation of His enemies.

Adina is the only other character that is developed in any depth. She begins the tale as a happy girl of seventeen, and, when it ends, she is a more mature maiden of twenty. This change is not remarkable considering what Adina saw and experienced, but one flaw in the novel is that Ingraham seldom lets the reader know that time is passing. Adina goes through a believable series of changes in relation to Jesus, but readers are generally not aware of the time it takes to effect these changes. She first has doubts, and later she believes; when Jesus is captured, her faith wavers and dies with Him. When Jesus rises from the tomb, her faith returns and does not waver again; indeed, after the Resurrection Adina is very contrite about her doubts. Her rhetorical excesses are displayed in some previously quoted passages and are those of a typical Ingraham romantic heroine. Ingraham, however, does make her more believable than some female characters in his earlier novels because she does change as the novel progresses.

Adina is the "author" of the thirty-nine letters, but hers is not the only point of view employed. She often quotes accounts and letters of others who are in a position to observe more than she. The disciple John, for instance, is quoted at length on Jesus' capture and trial while Mary, Adina's cousin, writes to Martha and Lazarus another view of the same momentous events. None of the different accounts, however, vary greatly in style.

It is often difficult to maintain complete organic unity in an epistolary novel, and *Prince* illustrates this fact well. Ingraham characteristically spends much time and space with minute descriptions of actions and places. One testimony to the novel's lack of unity is provided by the 1948 edition published by the London firm of Collins. An editor has cut out about twenty percent of the lengthy novel, and that unknown editor's deletions seldom do violence to Ingraham's story. As has been mentioned, Ingraham revised the book himself, but his revisions were relatively minor. He corrected some place names ("Bethany" instead of "Bethlehem") and slightly altered the structure of some sentences through the addition or deletion of dependent clauses. The 1855 edition uses more exclamation marks for emphasis than does the later edition, and the first edition is extremely irregular in capitalizing pronouns referring to Jesus, slips largely rectified by 1859. The biggest substantive change in Ingraham's second edition was that he omitted the postscript at the end of the last letter which explains what later happened to Adina.

Prince was almost certainly popular for its content as well as for its form. It told an absorbing tale in the nonbiblical language familiar to the nineteenth-century reading public. One critic has correctly noted that Ingraham's nonintellectualized treatment of Jesus and his emphasis on Jesus' miracles were exactly what a mass audience was waiting for.[3] The novel creates genuine suspense and maintains interest even though the reader already knows the outcome of Jesus' life. Much emphasis is placed on action, and, though the novel is classified as romantic, it does have realistic touches about such items as Jesus' sufferings, the envy of the priests, and Adina's wavering faith.

I *Israel in Bondage*

In contrast, *The Pillar of Fire* (1859), Ingraham's second biblical novel, is neither as interesting nor as suspenseful. *Pillar,* which is based on the Old Testament account of the Hebrew bondage in Egypt as found in Exodus, enlarges the brief biblical account to six hundred pages. Ingraham set the beginning of his novel in 1581 B.C., and ended it forty-six years later. An epistolary novel, *Pillar* contains forty-four letters by four different authors. The major correspondent is Sesostris, the twenty-eight-year-old prince of Tyre, who goes to Egypt to learn about the culture of the world's most powerful country.

The twenty-five letters written by Sesostris to his mother, Queen Epiphia, comprise the bulk of the novel. Sesostris' letters also have the least to do with the biblical source, although he does meet Remeses-Moses by his second letter. Sesostris is quite impressed with Egypt and gives an overview of attractions that he will examine later in more detail:

Egypt, compared with the kingdom of Phoenicia seems truly the land of the blessed. What far-famed warriors! what stately priests, clothed with power from the gods! What superb princes! . . . what grace and dignity in the virgins of the Sun! what a stupendous system of worship! what mighty mausoleums, both tomb and temple, rising like mountains hewn into solid triangles everywhere over the illimitable plain! What a land of verdure and of flowers!—land of gardens and palaces, obelisks and fountains, fanes and altars, sphinxes and gigantic statues!—land, comprising all that can delight the heart or take captive the sense! (26-27)

Most of Sesostris' letters concern the wonders of Egypt. Just as *Prince* illustrates Ingraham's technique through its love plot, *Pillar* reveals the early travel writer through the mass of travel commentary that takes up over half the novel. Some of the commentary is entertaining, but, in the interest of organic unity, most of it could be omitted.

One point where the novel differs from the Bible is that, according to Ingraham, Egypt is ruled by Amense, Moses' mother. There is no Pharaoh, and Remeses-Moses is heir to the throne. The future Pharaoh, however, wishes his mother long life because he does not want the problem of dealing with the ever-multiplying Hebrew slaves. The slaves are used to make brick for Egyptian building projects, and the Phoenician prince comments in his sixth letter that "this cruel bondage of the Hebrews is the only dark spot which I have seen in Egypt" (110). In this letter are scattered comments about the Hebrews juxtaposed against the marvels of Egypt.

Moeris, nephew of Amense, is second in line for the throne of Egypt; a subplot revolves around the rivalry between Moeris and Remeses-Moses. In terms of emphasis, the story of Moses almost qualifies as a subplot until the twenty-first letter. At that point Amense wants to give Moses the throne on his upcoming thirty-fifth birthday. Amense reveals that Moses is a Hebrew and was taken from the Nile in a basket of reeds. This revelation renews the reader's interest in the novel, and the Moses story dominates the latter third of the novel.

Because he is a Hebrew, Moses refuses to take the throne. The disappointment kills Amense, and Moeris becomes Pharaoh. Moses goes to Tyre with Sesostris, and Sesostris' letters end. Moses writes a few letters to his brother Aaron and his sister Miriam, but it is Aaron who writes Sesostris that Moses returned to Egypt and killed an Egyptian who was beating a Hebrew. Moses flees, and forty years pass before the action is resumed.

Remeses, prince of Tyre and of Damascus, son of King Sesostris, visits Egypt after the forty years and writes his father the eleven remaining letters of the novel. Moeris is dead; Thothmeses IV is Pharaoh. Remeses decides to visit Midian and meet Moses, who has been tending sheep and writing the book of Genesis. Remeses, of course, has come at an important time, for Moses soon discovers that he is to deliver the Hebrews out of their Egyptian bondage.

Moses leaves Midian, goes to Egypt, and presents God's demand for the Hebrews' freedom to the Pharaoh. The ruler's stubbornness and the consequent plagues follow rather closely chapters 7 through 12 of Exodus, though Ingraham does add details to the brief biblical account. The Hebrews leave Egypt, cross the Arabian Sea on dry land, and see God drown the entire Egyptian army. Moses goes upon Mount Sinai and receives God's Ten Commandments with remarkably little authorial fanfare or detail. He returns to find the fickle Hebrews dancing naked around a gold model of Serapis, one of the Egyptian gods modeled for them by Aaron. Moses calls on the faithful to slay the idolaters, and three thousand Hebrews die. Moses tells Remeses that the people will have to spend years in the wilderness for worshipping an idol, and so Remeses joins a passing caravan and returns home at the end of the novel.

Ingraham, in an appendix to *Pillar*, shows that he did his historical homework. He explains where he gathered most of the detail about Egypt that fills much of his novel. He also indicates that his purpose in writing *Pillar* was similar to his purpose for *Prince:* ". . . to draw the attention of those persons who do not read the Bible, or who read it carelessly, to the wonderful events it records, as well as the divine doctrine it teaches; and to tempt them to seek the inspired sources from which he mainly draws his facts" (600). Ingraham does take some facts from the Bible and is generally faithful to the tale of the deliverance of the Hebrews from Egypt, but—as his appendix indicates and the novel confirms—he certainly did not take all his facts from that source. As far as "divine doctrine" is concerned, he does not teach except obliquely, a trait *Pillar* shares with *Prince*. One reviewer commented that the book "makes use of the known customs of the people and the times. . . . The style is highly ornate, perhaps a little to [sic] plethoric for a severe taste. . . . It may be safely commended, as contributing to a larger knowledge both of Israel in bondage and his Egyptian oppressors,—and as the author hopes—it may lead to a more careful study of their history in the Book of Books."[4] Ingraham attempts to create suspense here as he did in *Prince* by sprinkling throughout his letters cryptic bits of news that he expands later on, but the technique is not as effective here because of the masses of historical data. Both the epistolary form and the historical data work effectively against the unity of the novel.

Ingraham ends his appendix and the volume by announcing the subject of his next novel: "The author's plan embraces three works of equal size. They cover the three great eras of Hebrew history, viz.: its beginning, at the Exodus; its culmination, as in the reigns of David and Solomon; its decline, as in the day of our Lord's incarnation" (600). The next novel of the author's trilogy, then, would cover "the reigns of David and Solomon."

Though *Pillar* is narrated by four letter writers, there are no stylistic differences between the correspondents. Ingraham stays out of the novel, but his first-person narrators all have the tendency to digress from the main subject, a trait exhibited in most of the writer's novels. Indeed, it is these digressions that take up most of *Pillar*. Sesostris warns his mother that "you must not, in familiar letters, look for artistic continuity of narrative" (55), and the reader certainly notices little. Some readers, however, would enjoy the digressions on Egyptian culture, for they tell much about the general period around 1581 B.C. because the details are accurate and not figments of the author's imagination.

The characters are not well-developed. Moses, even before he finds he is a Hebrew, is disposed to kindness toward the slaves and belief in one god though it is not the God of the Hebrews. The discovery of his birth changes only his situation, not his character; Sesostris enjoys acquiring new knowledge and is loyal to Moses before and after the Hebrew blood tie is announced. Sesostris is betrothed to a princess, but the novel is surprisingly devoid of a love plot. Queen Amense is the only other character drawn at any length, and she is simply a just, wise queen who dearly loves her adopted son.

In spite of its faults, *Pillar* was a popular novel. It sold nearly 500,000 copies in six months,[5] and its continued popularity is suggested by the fact that it was often reprinted after Ingraham's death. The popularity of these biblical novels helped lead Ingraham to produce his next novel within a year.

II *The Story of King David*

The Throne of David, the third of Ingraham's trilogy on the history of the Hebrews, was dated from Holly Springs, Mississippi, on January 26, 1860. Its six hundred pages constitute a picture of the second great period of Hebrew history, the reigns of King Saul and King David. Like its predecessors, *Throne* is an epistolary novel which considerably amplifies the biblical narrative. It is narrated in eighteen letters—sixteen by Arbaces, cousin of Belus, king of Assyria, and two by Hadad Ben Isrilid, Arbaces' son. In all, the novel covers about forty-three years, the last three years of Saul's reign and the forty years of David's.

King Belus dispatches his cousin Arbaces to Egypt with his

proposal to marry Pharaoh's daughter. So, around 1050 B.C., Arbaces leaves for Egypt on his mission with a huge retinue. He has to pass through the kingdom of the Hebrews on his way and pens his first letter from the city of Jericho, near the Jordan River. Arbaces reports that the prophet Samuel no longer rules the Hebrews; King Saul does. The ambassador meets Jonathan, son of Saul, and is greatly impressed by the young prince. Arbaces also meets the aged Samuel as well as the young shepherd David. To complete his acquaintance with the most important people of the day, Arbaces finally meets Saul,

the most magnificent looking man I ever beheld! Tall, with almost the proportions of a splendid giant; yet, from the perfect symmetry of his limbs, carrying himself with a firm, graceful, and noble air! His head was grand! and covered with short masses of curling locks, which were black as night! . . . He seemed to be about fifty-six or eight years of age, a few silver threads woven into his heavy beard, which covered only his upper lip and cheeks. (155-56)

Despite his imposing appearance, Saul is often visited with an incurable gloominess that erases much of his magnificence. This moodiness is God's judgment on Saul, for the king had once offered a sacrifice before battle without the presence of a priest. For his impiety, Saul is told that he is the last of his line that will remain upon the throne of Israel.

While Arbaces is at Saul's court, the king has to war against the Phillistines. Goliath of Gath, a nine-foot giant, challenges Saul to combat, but the king is seized with one of his moods and cannot fight. The young shepherd David stuns Goliath with a stone and cuts off the giant's head. Proclaimed a hero by the people, David only manages to enrage Saul, and the king makes an attempt on the shepherd's life. David flees the court. When David leaves, Arbaces, after three months in Judea, heads again for Egypt.

The ambassador arrives in Egypt and woos Zaila, Pharaoh's daughter, for Belus. Zaila, however, falls in love with Arbaces and says she will marry only him. The ambassador refuses and is thrown into prison for his allegiance to his king's interests. Arbaces spends two and a half years in prison and is released only when Zaila dies. He returns to Judea and writes Belus about the failure of his trip.

David has become a greater hero to the people since Arbaces

left for Egypt. While Arbaces languishes in the Egyptian prison, Saul and his son Jonathan die on the battlefield, and David is crowned king of Israel. When the ambassador returns to Israel, King David asks him to stay at court as resident Assyrian ambassador. Arbaces adopts the Hebrew faith, marries the Jewess Adora, and prepares to remain at David's court.

When the story resumes, seven years have passed. David has been attempting to unify the Hebrews and has spent much of his reign on the battlefield. Adora is heiress to the throne of Tadmor and, since David wants the kingdom in friendly hands, he deposes an usurper, and Adora is crowned queen; Arbaces is then prince-consort.

Twenty years pass before the story begins anew. David has stopped worshipping God since he has all he desires. Hadad Ben Isrilid, son of Arbaces and Adora, comes to Jerusalem to learn "the art of arms and of letters" (519) and begins the first of two letters to his parents. David has slipped so far that he has gotten Bathsheba, wife of the soldier Uriah, pregnant. He orders Uriah home from war to cover up his transgression, but his strategem fails. David then orders Uriah put in the forefront of battle, and the warrior is slain. David marries Bathsheba. The prophet Nathan rebukes the king who confesses his guilt; the illegitimately conceived child dies as a measure of God's displeasure.

Seven more years pass. Solomon, another son, has been born to David and Bathsheba. After a few comments on the state of the kingdom, Isrilid ends his last letter and returns to Tadmor. Ingraham tells his readers that Solomon followed David and that Solomon erected the temple to God that David was prevented from building by continued warfare. Ingraham also lists the books of the Old Testament from which he drew his story— Joshua, 1 Samuel, 2 Samuel, and 1 Kings. Four appendices explain some aspects of Solomon's reign.

Throne, like *Pillar* and *Prince,* was written to entertain and to draw the reader back to his Bible. The author notes that his purpose of sending people to the Bible had been successful. He reports that he had received "numerous letters . . . from grateful writers" (8) who had redirected their attention to the Bible. Obviously his public found the stories entertaining, for they were certainly read.

If the reader goes to the Bible after reading *Throne* however, he will discover that Ingraham made a few minor changes that help to illustrate his conception of the temper of the time. Arbaces' trip and his love for Adora give some continuity to the whole, but their story is not in the Scriptures. Ingraham added other fictional incidents to the "facts" reported in the Bible, but in *Throne*, unlike in the other two biblical novels, he changed some facts to fit his story.

According to Ingraham, when Saul learned that David wished to marry his daughter Michal, Saul required that David bring him the heads of one hundred Philistines. David brought him two hundred heads and claimed his bride. According to the Bible, Saul required the foreskins of one hundred Philistines, and David brought him two hundred. Another instance where Ingraham took some liberty occurs when Amnon, one of David's sons, "insulted his sister, Tamar, in a manner no brother could lightly pardon" (555). The Bible in 2 Samuel 13:14 reports that Amnon raped Tamar. In both instances, however, Tamar was avenged by Absalom, who killed Amnon. It is apparent that Ingraham felt explicit references to sexual matters had no place in his novel, or, perhaps, he felt that his method of enlarging upon the original would simply not have been accepted by the reading public in these cases. He had to mention David's seduction of Bathsheba to explain the later presence of Solomon, but, at least, in that instance, the fruit of the seduction died as punishment for the deed. Solomon was born after David and Bathsheba were lawfully married.

Throne has much descriptive material which could have been omitted. Most of the novel uses a vocabulary and diction common to other Ingraham stories, a language aimed at being plainly understood. *Throne* contains several unacknowledged passages quoted from the Bible that stand out because their vocabulary is different. One biblical passage quoted almost verbatim occurs when God speaks to Moses just before he dies and says " 'This is the land which I sware unto Abraham, unto Isaac, and unto Jacob, saying, I will give it unto thy seed! Behold, this land of Canaan I give unto the children of Israel for a possession forever! Lo, I have caused thee to see it with thine eyes but thou shalt not go over thither!' " (57). In Deuteronomy 34:4 (King James version) the passage reads: "This *is* the land which I sware unto Abraham, unto Isaac, and unto Jacob, saying, I will give it unto thy seed: I have caused thee to see *it* with thine eyes, but thou shalt not go over thither." The changes are minimal. Ingraham primarily added a sentence and some exclamation marks. In forthright narrative his speakers do not use such biblical forms as "thy," "thee," or "thou." They use the "your" and "you" with which a nineteenth-century reader would feel more comfortable.

Four narrators tell the story—Arbaces, Hadad, Heleph, and Ingraham himself. Heleph, who was an armor bearer to Jonathan, wrote to Arbaces when the latter was in an Egyptian prison. Ingraham added details to the story that Arbaces could not or does not. The author's main contribution occurs when Arbaces is in prison. The first-person point of view does give the reader a sense of participating directly in the action, but the technique would have been more effective if each narrator had distinct differences.

With the possible exception of David, the characters are not well-developed. David is, first, a shepherd. He soon becomes Saul's favorite harper, then a champion of the people. David is crowned king, wins many victories, forgets the Lord, and seduces Bathsheba. He is then penitent and later shows forbearance when his son Absalom tries to depose him. Through these changes we do see several facets of the man and learn of his strengths as well as his frailties. Because he is revealed as a human and not as a perfect being, he is certainly the most believable person in the novel.

III *The Circle Closes*

Although *The Throne of David* was Ingraham's final novel, it was not his last printed work. Ingraham ended his publishing career as he had begun it—by writing of the South, its customs, and its inhabitants. *The Sunny South,* printed in the latter part of 1860[6], was a collection of sixty-nine letters written by "Kate Conyngham" and addressed to the editor of the Philadelphia *Saturday Courier.* Most of the letters were printed in the *Courier* and appeared at intervals from 1853 through 1856 (4).

Ingraham, who professed to editing the volume, wrote an "Editorial Letter" to George G. Evans, the original printer, in which he noted that "Thirty years' residence at the South, chiefly at Natchez, Nashville, and Mobile, enables me to form, perhaps, a correct estimate of the accuracy of a work professing to relate the experiences of a stranger from the North" (3). The "stranger" is Kate Conyngham who, at age nineteen, leaves a village not far from Portland, Maine, to become a governess to Isabel Peyton, who lives two and a half hours' ride from Nashville, Tennessee. *The Sunny South* tells us what Kate saw and experienced in this Southern city.

Though *The Sunny South* does have a plot of sorts in telling what happens to Kate over a five-year period, the volume is also a travel narrative. It differs from *The South-West* in having that faint plot, in using somewhat less description, and in being much more sentimental and defensive about the Southern way of life. The defensiveness is partly indicated in Ingraham's statement that

> The tone of the Book is strictly conservative and national, . . . [it] will, without doubt, be an acceptable gift to the reading public; especially, when hitherto so much in relation by our people and institutions is misunderstood and misinterpreted by those who have no personal knowledge either of Southerners or of Southern life. . . .
> The object of this work is to do justice to the Southern planter, and, at the same time, afford information in an agreeable form to the Northerner. (4-5)

Despite a disclaimer, the book was written in answer to Harriet Beecher Stowe's *Uncle Tom's Cabin* (1852). Ingraham had offered *The Sunny South* to Fletcher Harper in 1855 and told him at that time that the volume was a reply to Mrs. Stowe.[7] There is nothing that Kate comments on so often and at such length as the place of slaves in Southern society.

Kate's sentimentality toward the slaves is evident in her musing on an inscription found on a tombstone erected for a faithful black by his master. Kate comments "'A faithful servant.' . . . Who can ask for greater commendation? In his narrow and humble sphere he served faithfully, and has entered into his rest. Oh! that I, also, may have it inscribed upon my tomb, that I have been 'a faithful servant' in my sphere wherein my Maker has placed me. It is praise enough for a king" (266). The reader will also find effusions on a pet deer, several horses, and assorted other animals. Signing the letters "Kate Conyngham" and infusing them with sentimentality may have been a calculated move by Ingraham to snare the female audience that Stowe had captured as well as to disguise their authorship by a man known to prefer Southern living.

Colonel Peyton's plantation is a large one that utilizes the services of many slaves. These blacks live in a neat village on the estate. Shortly after her arrival from Maine, Kate notes that

> I am already getting reconciled to slavery, since I find that it does not, in reality, exhibit the revolting horrors I was taught in the North to discover in it. There are many things to admire and to interest one in the social and domestic condition of the slaves, and I am almost ready to acknowledge that the African is happier in bondage than free! At least one thing is certain: nearly all the free negroes I have ever seen in the North were miserable creatures, poor, ragged, and often criminal. Here they are well clad, moral, nearly all religious, and the temptations that demoralize the free blacks in our northern cities are unknown to, and cannot approach them. (59)

The pleasant condition of the slaves and the kindness of their masters is mentioned again and again. Kate is even given a female slave to attend to her needs when she arrives in Tennessee.

Life on the Peyton plantation is fun. Kate goes fox hunting, deer hunting, and fishing, and sips an occasional mint julep. She reads often and occasionally comments on the transitory quality of literary fame. On one visit to Nashville she notes that "The churches of this city are not handsome or imposing. And who do you suppose I heard read the service, the last Sabbath I was in town? Mr. H—, once an author, who has been for two years past studying for orders in the church. He is also principal of an Academy for young ladies in the city, a position which he holds temporarily, until he shall be ordained. I trust he will be eminently useful as a clergyman" (74). It is fair to say that Ingraham was "eminently useful as a clergyman."

Kate visits a spa in Columbia, Tennessee, and, after some time with the family, goes with them on a trip to New Orleans, where Colonel Peyton expects to sell his cotton and tobacco. They board the steamer *America* at Nashville and travel the Cumberland River north to where it joins the Ohio and, finally, the Mississippi. The fifteen-hundred mile trip is interrupted by a brief stay in Natchez at a plantation that obviously is modeled on that belonging to Ingraham's mother-in-law. Kate tells us that six letters about the trip from Nashville to Natchez were lost in the mail and not rewritten, leaving some gap in the continuity of her travels. The party stops at a sugar plantation north of New Orleans and Isabel, Kate's pupil, is soon engaged to the son of the owner. The couple is married, and Kate accompanies them by ship to New York, where they leave for Europe while Kate returns to Maine.

Two years pass before Kate writes another letter. She is now Mrs. de Cressy and lives on a sugar plantation in Thibodeau, Louisiana. The letters become even more sentimental as Kate writes about her husband, her home, and her new son. Kate does not forget slavery however. This set of letters displays an awareness that the country's difference in attitudes on slavery is becoming dangerous to the Union. She reports that "So great is the hostility of the northern abolitionists against the South, that southern parents are becoming more and more reluctant to send their sons and daughters there" to school (494-95). Unless "Abolitionism cease its hostility, the South will separate itself from the North" (495). Kate does believe in the ways of her adopted region, but she is also for the Union and regrets the interference of Northern abolitionists in the South's affairs.

Kate travels after she is married, but the descriptions of her journeys are not detailed. She goes to Mobile and heads northeast through Montgomery, Alabama, Augusta, Georgia, and on through the Carolinas. The volume ends as she and her family are preparing to leave New York for a two-year sojourn in England.

The Sunny South is a superficial travel volume when compared to the detailed travel sketches in *The South-West*. *The Sunny South* seems to have been written primarily for the women of the nineteenth century. Its sentimentality would not have gained it many male readers. The two works are an indication, however, of how much Ingraham had come to love the South in the twenty-five years that separated their publication. *The South-West* is not only detailed, but it is also relatively straightforward, unbiased travel writing. *The Sunny South* is more domestic in its emphasis and more emphatically favorable to the ways of the region. Both books have value as works which display various facets of the antebellum South. The South was a region of some leisure and much less complexity than the North. People may have been just as poor in the South as in the North, but Ingraham shows more unhappiness and more evil coming from the land of the Yankee as the Northerners attempted to interfere in the life of another region.

Besides illustrating his love for his adopted region, *The Sunny South* often shows the feelings of the minister who wrote it. Kate frequently quotes and makes specific references to Bible verses as she moves through her daily life. She gives a lengthy account of how a slave saw Jesus and was converted. She is quite humanitarian and comments once that she abhors capital punishment and that life imprisonment would be an improvement over the death penalty. She reads and enjoys Emerson's "Nature" but does not understand how Emerson could not believe the New Testament.

Obviously, Ingraham's career as a minister did indeed influence the content of his works though it did not much influence his techniques. He began and ended his literary career by printing volumes about the South he loved and adopted, but the focus of the works is different. *The South-West* describes rather straightforwardly and with little prejudice a region known by comparatively few. *The Sunny South* de-emphasizes the travel material and stresses the pleasantness of the South and its institutions. All of the biblical novels display the interest in travel description that marked *The South-West,* but they show less of the romantic influence found in the brief romantic novels that held the fancy of the reading public in the 1840s. It was the subject matter of the biblical novels that marked the last phase in Ingraham's writing career as different. But when one considers the religious overtones in several of his earlier works, he cannot be too surprised that Ingraham would use the Bible as source material for several novels.

At the time of his death Ingraham was apparently planning to lengthen his story of Elfrida into a fourth biblical novel, *St. Paul the Roman Citizen,* and to reduce his ministerial duties so he would be able to devote more time to "'preaching through books.'"[8] He would have been well-pleased to continue his career as a writer of biblical fiction, for in it he was able to combine the travel description and romance so characteristic of most of his work. Also, he was again able, with those last novels, to write works that were comparable in length or longer than those written early in his career. With only a few changes in subject matter, therefore, Ingraham would have been able to continue a career he had so strongly begun over twenty-five years earlier.

CHAPTER 7

Epilogue

THERE is no need to exaggerate Joseph Holt Ingraham's literary abilities, for he is clearly not a major writer. His significance lies in his historical importance; he was a child of his times and a mirror of some aspects of it. His work is of interest, if only as a contrast to contemporary writing of genuine literary merit. Not every fiction writer of Ingraham's era was on a level with Poe, Hawthorne, or Melville—but these men were not widely read and appreciated in their lifetimes. Ingraham, however, was read both during his time and after it, though his fame was ephemeral, and the curtains of oblivion are now hard to part.

Much is now known about Ingraham, but the missing data on his life would still fill a respectable essay; a definitive bibliography of his works may always remain impossible. Though he preferred to be thought of as a Southern writer, most of his works had Northern settings and were printed above the Mason-Dixon line. The reasons are obvious—book production and distribution in the North were more coordinated and allowed for a wider number of readers.

Ingraham aimed his volumes at the masses, but the masses are fickle, and as society changed in the Gilded Age so did its preferences, and Ingraham's works, except for the biblical novels, were largely ignored. The sheer bulk of his writing and its lack of availability also work against his finding an audience today.

Whatever his faults—and Ingraham certainly had many—he could tell a good story. His tales may not be abstract or philosophical but, at their best, they have a physical virility, a directness in portrayal of people, places, and events that is praiseworthy. He is no Hawthorne, but neither is he one of the "damn mob of scribbling women" who usually wallowed in

Epilogue

sentimentalism and propriety. Perhaps the cornerstone of his work is his ability to delineate small facts and events so clearly that an often convincing reality springs from them. His *Lafitte* may be melodramatic, but the pirate lives; Ingraham may be scored for his tendency to overdo the didactic, but most authors also employed that characteristic in a age which still had lingering doubts about the propriety of the novel. He often used stock characters, but his portrayals of city "sports," Southern colonels, Maine sea captains, Negroes, and Jews were not lifeless.

Faced today with an abundance of excellent present and past literary work, modern readers have a tendency to view popular writers of the past as insignificant and superficial. They forget that the clichés often found in such writing may not have been trite to a contemporary audience, that their presentations were often viewed as original, not repetitive—at least by enough people to make Ingraham a writer to be reckoned with in his lifetime. For all his success, Ingraham did not make much money from his writings, though he did receive "the everlasting gratitude of his publishers"[1] and a vast audience. It would be most interesting to know how much his publishers profited. Roberts Brothers bought the stereotype plates and copyrights of Ingraham's three biblical romances in 1863 and kept the novels in print constantly through 1898. They made "tremendous profits" on the volumes.[2] The Williams brothers must have also profited, but none of their records survive.

Ingraham's two major Southern contemporaries are Poe and Simms, but the field boasts many writers that are not of the first rank. Both Poe and Ingraham were prolific writers; both experienced financial troubles during their lifetimes. Ingraham wrote almost as much as Simms, though Simms' work is decidedly more regional. Simms and Ingraham were aware of each other, but whether they ever met or corresponded has not been fully investigated. Students of American literature, particularly of the South, may find it worthwhile to compare the lives and work of these three authors and so gain a better understanding of the period in which they worked.

Ingraham was a pioneer in the biblical novel, in periodical publications, and in tales of miscegenation. He was a precursor of Horatio Alger, and the intermittent realism in such tales as *Frank Rivers,* "West Point," *The Miseries of New York,* and *Burton* deserves comparisons with later, more skilled writers. His use of dialect should be compared with that of other regional authors.

Ingraham wrote about what was right about America when he wrote of the Revolution and the correctness of our cause in such a tale as *Neal Nelson. Charles Blackford* and other stories pointed out that our society had its faults. Ingraham believed strongly in morality, that both correct behavior and lapses would be justly rewarded. His views may be regarded as simplistic by people today who hold few beliefs with such assurance.

Ingraham had talent, although it was a limited and undisciplined talent. He began his work with industry and was phenomenally busy at it for twelve years before he began to study for the ministry. Then his writing became an avocation, not a business, and when the number of his works dropped drastically, his fame, ironically, grew brighter. He was apparently going to return to writing as a vocation when death intervened.

Would Ingraham have accomplished more had he lived longer? He would have undoubtedly written more, but its quality would probably not have improved, for his early subjects and propensities, once established, were not altered greatly. Ingraham was not a John Keats whose untimely passing is mourned for what might have been. Yet his works remain of primary value to the literary and cultural historian and deserve continued study.

Notes and References

Chapter One

1. It must be remembered, however, that the directories list only heads of households and are not totally reliable. The Portland papers of the 1809-1810 era did not carry birth announcements.

2. *Maine. A History. Biographical* (New York: American Historical Society, 1919), p. 118.

3. Albert Johannsen, *The House of Beadle and Adams and Its Dime and Nickel Novels. The Story of a Vanished Literature* (Norman: University of Oklahoma Press, 1950), II, 151.

4. *Portland Gazette and Maine Advertiser*, August 25, 1806 [p. 3].

5. Ibid., June 12, 1809, p. 4.

6. Ibid., January 27, 1818, p. 4.

7. Ibid., July 30, 1822, p. 2.

8. Harlowe Harris, *The Portland Directory, for the Year 1841* (Portland: Arthur Shirley and Son, 1841), p. 51; the Portland city directories for 1844, 1846, 1847, and 1852 list James as being in Portland. His name is absent in 1856.

9. Portland *Eastern Argus*, June 4, 1856, p. 2.

10. *Biographical Memoranda Respecting All Who Ever Were Members of the Class of 1832 in Yale College* (New Haven: Yale University, 1860), p. 167.

11. Johannsen, II, 151.

12. Letter, Ingraham to Rev. Jeremiah Day, June 29, 1828. Ms. owned by the Beinecke Rare Book and Manuscript Library of Yale University and printed with their permission.

13. Letter, Judith A. Schiff, Chief Research Archivist, Yale University Library, to author, April 2, 1973.

14. Letter, Ingraham to Rev. Jeremiah Day, February 21, 1830. Ms. owned by the Beinecke Rare Book and Manuscript Library of Yale University and printed with their permission. The present writer cannot explain why this letter, among those that survive, is so filled with common grammatical errors.

15. Letter, Kenneth C. Cramer, Archives Department, Baker Memorial Library, Dartmouth College, to author, February 19, 1973.

16. Johannsen, II, 151.

17. Johannsen, II, 151; David H. Bishop, "Joseph Holt Ingraham,"

Library of Southern Literature, ed. Edwin Anderson Alderman and Joel Chandler Harris (New Orleans: Martin and Hoyt Company, 1907), VI, 2591; D. Clayton James, *Antebellum Natchez* (Baton Rouge: Louisiana State University Press, 1968), p. 143, says Ingraham joined the faculty in 1830. The editor of the Natchez *Mississippi Free Trader*, in a December 24, 1860, obituary (p. 2), notes that Ingraham was a professor in 1830-1831. Jay B. Hubbell, *The South in American Literature, 1607-1900* (Durham: Duke University Press, 1954), p. 623, says that Ingraham did not join the faculty of Jefferson College until 1832. According to *The South-West*, Ingraham did not arrive in Natchez until December 1830, making Hubbell's estimate appear more nearly correct, especially if Ingraham did indeed dabble in law and business before turning to teaching.

18. In March 1973, the present writer examined the records of Jefferson College that still exist in the Mississippi Department of Archives and History. No mention of Ingraham could be found. The *Natchez Daily Courier*, May 27, 1857, p. 2, contains a reference to the days of Ingraham at Jefferson College. The *Mississippi Free Trader and Natchez Tri-Weekly Gazette*, June 8, 1837, p. 2, refers to Ingraham as "late of Jefferson College."

19. Charles S. Sydnor, *A Gentleman of the Old Natchez Region: Benjamin L. C. Wailes* (Durham: Duke University Press, 1938), p. 133.

20. The *Natchez*, November 13, 1830, p. 364.

21. The *Natchez*, May 25, 1832, p. 167.

22. Warren Graham French, "A Sketch of the Life of Joseph Holt Ingraham," *Journal of Mississippi History* 11 (July 1949): 159.

23. *Natchez Courier: and Adams, Jefferson and Franklin Advertiser*, August 23, 1833, p. 3.

24. Eino Railo, *The Haunted Castle. A Study of the Elements of English Romanticism* (1927; rpt. New York: Humanities Press, 1964), p. 315.

25. Letter, Ingraham to Harper & Brothers, May 29, 1839. Later references to the amounts Ingraham received from the Harpers come from this letter.

26. Edgar Allan Poe, Rev. of *The South-West*, *Southern Literary Messenger* 2 (January 1836): 122-23.

27. C. Hugh Holman, *The Roots of Southern Writing, Essays on the Literature of the American South* (Athens: University of Georgia Press, 1972), p. 76.

28. Earl L. Bradsher, "Book Publishers and Publishing," *The Cambridge History of American Literature*, ed. William Peterfield Trent et al. (New York: Macmillan Co., 1946), III, 549.

29. William Charvat, *Literary Publishing in America: 1790-1850* (Philadelphia: University of Pennsylvania Press, 1859), p. 94.

30. Eugene Exman, *The Brothers Harper. A Unique Publishing*

Partnership and Its Impact upon the Cultural Life of America from 1817-1853 (New York: Harper & Row, 1965), p. 94.

31. William Charvat, *The Profession of Authorship in America, 1800-1870*, ed. Matthew J. Bruccoli (Columbus: Ohio State University Press, 1968), p. 3.

32. French, p. 159.

33. Letter, Ingrahame [sic] to William A. Coleman, July 28, 1835.

34. Edgar Allan Poe, Rev. of *Lafitte: The Pirate of the Gulf*, *Southern Literary Messenger* 2 (August 1836): 593-96.

35. Alexander Cowie, *The Rise of the American Novel* (New York: American Book Co., 1948), p. 289.

36. Charvat, *Literary Publishing in America*, p. 66.

37. "The Theatre," *Ladies' Companion* 5 (August 1836): 202.

38. Contract, Ingraham and Harper & Brothers, September 29, 1836.

39. *Burton* (New York: Harper & Brothers, 1838), I, x.

40. Chester Whitney Wright, *Economic History of the United States* (New York: McGraw-Hill Book Co., Inc., 1949), pp. 385-87; Exman, p. 92.

41. Holman, pp. 78, 79.

42. Contract, Ingraham and Harper & Brothers, September 29, 1836; Exman, p. 99.

43. Federal Writers Project, *Mississippi: A Guide to the Magnolia State* (New York: Viking Press, 1938), p. 334.

44. September 8, 1838, p. 174.

45. Henry Wadsworth Longfellow, *Life of Henry Wadsworth Longfellow*, ed. Samuel Longfellow (Boston: Houghton, Mifflin and Company, 1891), I, 312.

46. Contract, Ingraham and Harper & Brothers, October 16, 1838.

47. *Eastern Argus*, December 19, 1849, p. 2; October 31, 1859, p. 3; J. S. Jones, *Captain Kyd; or the Wizard of the Sea. A Drama—In Four Acts* (Boston: William V. Spencer, n.d. [1856]), p. 2.

48. *Ladies' Companion* 10 (February 1839): 200.

49. Contract, Ingraham and Harper & Brothers, January 17, 1839.

50. Letter, Ingrahame [sic] to Edward Carey, April 6, 1839.

51. Letter, Ingrahame to Harper & Brothers, May 29, 1839. Ms. owned by Harper & Row and reprinted with their permission. Nothing is known of B. J. Ingraham except what is mentioned in this letter.

52. Letter, Ingrahame [sic] to Mrs. Ann S. Stephens, July 5, 1839.

53. *Southern Literary Messenger* 4 (September 1839): 631.

54. Letter, Ingraham to J. J. Smith, November 24, 1839.

55. Exactly who Ingraham's family consisted of at this time remains a matter of conjecture. There was his wife, of course; Laura, a daughter, was dead. A son, Prentiss, was born in 1843 and died in 1904. He surpassed his prolific father's efforts by writing over six hundred dime

novels and several plays. The parish records of Christ Church, Holly Springs, Mississippi, in 1860, the year of Ingraham's death, show that there was another son, Henry, and two daughters, Josephine and another Laura. When these last three children were born is unknown, and nothing is known about their lives.

56. Letter, Ingraham to Harper & Brothers, December 10, 1839. Ms. owned by Harper & Row and reprinted with their permission.

57. Letter, Ingraham to Fletcher Harper, January 31, 1840.

58. *Democratic Review* 6 (November 1839): 399-411; London: Richard Bentley, 1840.

59. Rev. of *The Quadroone; or, St. Michael's Day, Ladies' Companion* 15 (May 1841); Edgar Allan Poe, Rev. of *The Quadroone, Graham's Lady's and Gentleman's Magazine* 18 (June 1841): 296.

60. Edgar Allan Poe, *The Letters of Edgar Allan Poe*, ed. John Ward Ostrom (Cambridge: Harvard University Press, 1948), I, 170-71.

61. Edgar Allan Poe, *The Complete Works of Edgar Allan Poe*, ed. James A. Harrison (New York: Thomas Y. Crowell, 1902), XV, 188.

62. Letter, Ingraham to Daniel Webster, June 15, 1841. Ms. is in the National Archives in Washington.

63. Letter, Ingraham to W. H. Butterworth, August 21, 1841. Ms. owned by the New York Public Library and reprinted with their permission.

64. William Gilmore Simms, *The Letters of William Gilmore Simms*, ed. Mary C. Simms Oliphant, Alfred Taylor Odell, and T. C. Duncan Eaves (Columbia: University of South Carolina Press, 1952), I, 269-71.

65. Exman, p. 100.

66. Natalia Summers, comp., *Lists of Documents Relating to Special Agents of the Department of State, 1789-1906* (Washington, D.C.: National Archives, 1951), p. 86.

67. Letter, Ingraham to Messrs. Ketchum and Fessenden, November 7, 1843. Ms. owned by the Historical Society of Pennsylvania and reprinted with their permission.

68. Jacob Blanck, "Joseph Holt Ingraham," *Bibliography of American Literature*, IV (New Haven: Yale University Press, 1963), 463.

69. James D. Hart, *The Popular Book. A History of America's Literary Taste* (Los Angeles: University of California Press, 1961), pp. 98-99.

70. Letter, James Lawton, Curator of Manuscripts, Boston Public Library, to author, April 13, 1973.

71. As Blanck notes, IV, p. 459, it is possible that all Ingraham's novels have not been located.

72. Letter, Ingraham to Messrs. Ketchum and Fessenden, November 7, 1843. This law firm may have been handling Ingraham's creditors.

Ms. owned by the Historical Society of Pennsylvania and reprinted with their permission.
73. Charvat, *The Profession of Authorship in America*, p. 262.
74. Arthur Herman Wilson, *A History of the Philadelphia Theatre 1835-1855* (New York: Greenwood Press, 1968), p. 75.
75. *Eastern Argus*, March 22, 1845, p. 2.
76. Letter, Ingraham to J. B. Staples, April 3, 1846. Ms. owned by Haverford College and reprinted with their permission.
77. Longfellow, II, 35.
78. Hubbell, p. 623.

Chapter Two

1. Albert Johannsen, *The House of Beadle and Adams and Its Dime and Nickel Novels. The Story of a Vanished Literature* (Norman: University of Oklahoma Press, 1950), II, 152.
2. Warren Graham French, "A Sketch of the Life of Joseph Holt Ingraham," *Journal of Mississippi History* 11 (July 1949): 163. *Church Review, and Ecclesiastical Register* 14 (April 1861): p. 187, reported that Ingraham was confirmed by Bishop Whittingham of Maryland in Washington, D.C. J. P. T. Ingraham (1819-1904) wrote several books on theology during his career as a minister. One of his poems, entitled "Byron," appeared in the *Evergreen* 10 (March 1853): 87. Dr. Ingraham, perhaps following in the footsteps of his prolific brother, wrote a series of travel sketches for the *Churchman* in 1855 entitled "Life Notes in the West."
3. *Mississippi Free Trader and Natchez Gazette*, March 17, 1847, p. 2.
4. J. H. Ingraham, *Report Upon a Proposed System of Public Education, for the City of Nashville, Respectfully Addressed to its Citizens* (Nashville: W. F. Bang and Co., 1848), p. 18.
5. Rev. J. H. Ingraham, "Secrets of the Cells: or, Leaves From My Diary," *Ballou's Pictorial Drawing-Room Companion* 8 (March 17, 1855): 162. According to the New York *Evening Mirror* 7 (December 21, 1847): 2, Ingraham studied theology under Bishop J. H. Otey of the Diocese of Tennessee.
6. Letter, *Nashville True Whig*, May 8, 1849, p. 2. Most of the following discussion of Ingraham's life in Tennessee appeared originally in the present writer's article, "J. H. Ingraham and Tennessee: A Record of Social and Literary Contributions," *Tennessee Historical Quarterly* 34 (Fall 1975): 264-72, and is reprinted with the kind permission of the *Quarterly*.
7. *Nashville True Whig*, April 10, 1848, p. 3.
8. *Nashville Daily Gazette*, July 12, 1849, p. 2.

9. *Nashville Daily Gazette,* July 3, 1850, p. 3; *Nashville True Whig,* April 10, 1849, p. 3.

10. *Tennessee's Public Schools* (Arlington, Tenn.: Tennessee Congress of Parents and Teachers, Inc., 1938), pp. 23, 25.

11. *Report* (Nashville: W. F. Bang and Co., 1848), p. 3.

12. Letter, Ingraham to Horace Mann, June 27, 1848. Ms. owned by Massachusetts Historical Society and reprinted with their permission.

13. *Nashville Whig,* October 5, 1848, p. 2.

14. Letter, Ingraham to Horace Mann, November 1, 1848. Ms. owned by the Massachusetts Historical Society and reprinted with their permission.

15. *Tennessee's Public Schools,* p. 26.

16. "Secrets of the Cells," p. 210. The six weekly installments of "Secrets," running from March 17 to April 21, tell of Ingraham's work with the prisoners at Nashville. Though romanticized in tone and perhaps in some detail, they appear essentially accurate.

17. *Journal of the Proceedings of the Twenty-Second Annual Convention of the Clergy and Laity of the Protestant Episcopal Church, in the Diocese of Tennessee* (Columbia, Tenn.: Mitchell and Rainey, 1850), p. 24.

18. "Secrets of the Cells," p. 210. The records of the Tennessee State Penitentiary from 1847 through 1851 were checked by the present writer at the Tennessee State Library and Archives on August 24, 1973. The prison reports do not mention Ingraham, but they do verify several incidents (such as the outbreak of cholera) that he used in his "Secrets of the Cells."

19. Bishop J. H. Otey, "Address," *Journal of the Proceedings . . . Twenty-Second Annual Convention,* pp. 16-17.

20. *Nashville Daily Gazette,* October 30, 1849, p. 2.

21. *Journal of the Proceedings . . . Twenty-Second Annual Convention,* p. 23.

22. Frank Luther Mott, *Golden Multitudes: The Story of Best Sellers in the United States* (New York: R. R. Bowker Co., 1947), p. 308.

23. Don C. Seitz, "A Prince of Best Sellers," *Publisher's Weekly* 119 (February 21, 1931): 940.

24. *Nashville Daily Gazette,* December 13, 1850, p. 2.

25. *Church Review, and Ecclesiastical Register* 14 (April 1861): 187.

26. *Journal of the Proceedings of the Twenty-Fifth Annual Convention of the Protestant Episcopal Church, in the Diocese of Mississippi* (Natchez: Natchez Courier Book and Job Office, 1851), p. 43.

27. Aberdeen *Monroe Democrat,* August 20, 1851, p. 3.

28. Rev. James Lundy Sykes, *History of St. John's Parish. Aberdeen, Mississippi* (n.p. [Aberdeen, Mississippi], n.d.), p. 3.

29. "Mississippi. Aberdeen," *Spirit of Missions* 6 (December 1851): 504.

30. "Mississippi. Aberdeen," *Spirit of Missions* 17 (May 1852): 143-44.
31. "The Novelist Divine," *Mississippi Free Trader*, February 18, 1852, p. 1.
32. *Monroe Democrat*, March 10, 1852, p. 4.
33. Rev. J. H. Ingraham, "Mississippi. Aberdeen," *Spirit of Missions* 17 (May 1852): 144.
34. *Monroe Democrat*, March 10, 1852, p. 4.
35. *Monroe Democrat*, March 24, 1853, p. 3.
36. "Mississippi. Aberdeen," *Spirit of Missions* 18 (May 1853): 133.
37. Ibid.
38. Sykes, p. 6; Aberdeen, Mississippi *Weekly Independent*, February 5, 1853, p. 3.
39. *Weekly Independent*, September 3, 1853, p. 3.
40. Lucy Green Nelson, *St. John's Church, Mobile. A History* (Mobile: Jordan Printing Co., 1963), pp. 16, 19.
41. *Journal of the Proceedings of the Twenty-Third Annual Convention of the Protestant Episcopal Church, in the Diocese of Alabama* (Mobile: Benjamin, Farrow and Co., 1854), p. 17.
42. Edgar Legare Pennington, "The Ministry of Joseph Holt Ingraham in Mobile, Alabama," *Historical Magazine of the Protestant Episcopal Church* 26 (December 1957): 357.
43. *Natchez Weekly Courier*, May 3, 1854, p. 1.
44. *Eastern Argus*, April 18, 1853, p. 2. Several items had appeared under Ingraham's name since 1846; they could have been published, however, without his permission.
45. J. H. Ingraham, *The Sunny South* (1860; reprint ed., New York: Negro Universities Press, 1968), p. 4.
46. Warren G. French, "A Hundred Years of a Religious Best-Seller," *Western Humanities Review* 10 (Winter 1955-56): 45.
47. Pennington, pp. 357-58.
48. Langley Ingraham, "Memoirs of Rev. J. H. Ingraham," TS, May 23, 1930, p. 2. Seitz makes the unsupported and obviously incorrect statement that Ingraham made $30,000 from *Prince's* sales.
49. Pennington, p. 360.
50. *Natchez Daily Courier*, February 18, 1857, p. 2.
51. Letter, Ingraham to Fletcher Harper, March 17, 1857.
52. Letter, Ingraham to Fletcher Harper, March 23, 1857.
53. *Natchez Daily Courier*, May 12, 1857, p. 2.
54. Rev. J. L. Gay, "Tennessee. Mouth of Tellico and Loudon," *Spirit of Missions* 17 (October 1852): 317.
55. Bishop J. H. Otey, "Address," *Journal of the Proceedings of the Thirtieth Annual Convention of the Protestant Episcopal Church, in the Diocese of Tennessee* (Nashville: Bang, Walker and Co., 1858), p. 37.

56. Rt. Rev. William Mercer Green, *Memoirs of Rt. Rev. James Harvey Otey, D.D., LL.D., The First Bishop of Tennessee* (New York: James Pott and Co., 1885), p. 66.

57. Otey, pp. 37, 39, 41.

58. *Natchez Weekly Courier*, February 10, 1858, p. 1; February 4, 1858, p. 3; Letter, Ingraham to Fletcher Harper, April 12, 1858.

59. "Report of the Historiographer. Rev. Mr. Gay's Missions in East Tennessee, 1852 to 1854," *Journal of the Fifty-Ninth Annual Convention of the Church in the Diocese of Tennessee* (Sewannee, Tenn.: University of the South Press, 1891), p. 48.

60. *Mississippi Free Trader*, June 26, 1858, p. 2.

61. *Natchez Daily Courier*, June 15, 1858, p. 2; *Natchez Weekly Courier*, June 15, 1858, p. 3.

62. *Natchez Daily Courier*, July 14, 1858, p. 2.

63. Parish Register, Christ Church, Holly Springs, Mississippi, Vol. 7, p. 1.

64. Charles N. Dean, "'A Century Ago . . .'" (n.p. [Holly Springs, Mississippi], n.d.), p. 1.

65. *Natchez Weekly Courier*, September 21, 1859, p. 2.

66. *Mississippi Free Trader*, June 23, 1859, p. 4.

67. Letter, Ingraham to Mrs. Anne M. Hall, November 8, 1859. Ms. owned by Barrett Library, University of Virginia Library, and reprinted with their permission.

68. *The Sunny South*, p. 4.

69. Review of *The Throne of David*, by Rev. J. H. Ingraham, *Portland Transcript*, May 19, 1860, p. 3.

70. Sydnor, p. 133.

71. Aunt Rosie [Mrs. S. L. Falconer], "Last Days of the Rev. Dr. Ingraham," TS, p. 1.

72. French, "A Sketch of . . . Ingraham," p. 168.

73. *Churchman's Monthly Magazine* 3 (January-October 1856).

74. Aunt Rosie, p. 1.

75. Langley Ingraham, p. 2. French, in "A Sketch of . . . Ingraham," p. 169, indicates that some people have postulated that Ingraham committed suicide, possibly because he was in financial straits. The notion seemed incorrect to French (although he did not know about the publication of "Elfrida") and seems incorrect as well to the present writer because Ingraham had had financial difficulties before and had been able to surmount them. He may have been upset by Carleton's refusal, but he must have known that his public would prove the publisher's action injudicious. Had he contemplated suicide, he certainly would have managed it in such a way that he did not have to suffer the agony he did. Since there is a lack of contemporary evidence on the suicide theory, it should be forgotten as one more error perpetrated by earlier biographers.

76. *Mississippi Free Trader,* December 24, 1860, p. 2. This obituary was more specific than Prentiss Ingraham about the wound. It states that the ball inflicted "a severe wound in the right thigh, just below the crotch, and ranging upward lodged, it is supposed, in the hip and near the spinal column."
77. Aunt Rosie, p. 2.
78. Langley Ingraham, p. 2.

Chapter Three

1. William Charvat, *Literary Publishing in America: 1790-1850* (Philadelphia: University of Pennyslvania Press, 1959), p. 81.
2. Ibid., p. 41.
3. Edgar Allan Poe, Rev. of *The South-West, Southern Literary Messenger* 2 (January 1836): 122-23.
4. Eino Railo, *The Haunted Castle. A Study of the Elements of English Romanticism* (1927; reprint ed., New York: Humanities Press, 1964), pp. 226-28.
5. Alexander Cowie, *The Rise of the American Novel* (New York: American Book Co., 1948), p. 289.
6. Edwin W. Gaston, Jr., *The Early Novels of the Southwest* (Albuquerque: University of New Mexico Press, 1961), p. 45.
7. Edgar Allan Poe, Rev. of *Lafitte: The Pirate of the Gulf, Southern Literary Messenger* 2 (August 1836): 595.
8. T. F. Henderson, "Sir Walter Scott," *Cambridge History of English Literature,* XII, ed. A. W. Ward and A. R. Waller (New York: Macmillan Co., 1933), 20, 19.
9. Portland *Eastern Argus,* September 9, 1836, p. 2.
10. Letter, Ingraham to Harper & Brothers, May 29, 1839.
11. James D. Hart, *The Oxford Companion to American Literature* (New York: Oxford University Press, 1965), p. 444.
12. Letter, Ingraham to Harper & Brothers, May 29, 1839.
13. J. S. Jones, *Captain Kyd; or, the Wizard of the Sea. A Drama—in Four Acts* (Boston: William V. Spencer, 1845), p. 2.
14. Jacob Blanck, *Bibliography of American Literature,* IV (New Haven: Yale University Press, 1963), p. 462; J. H. Ingraham, "Romance of American History, No. III. The Hostile Governors," *United States Magazine, and Democratic Review* 6 (November 1839): 399-411.
15. James Joseph Kinney, in his "The Theme of Miscegenation in the American Novel to World War I," Diss. University of Tennessee 1972, p. 25, notes that Ingraham was one of the first Southern writers to use the miscegenation theme before 1850.
16. Edgar Allan Poe, Rev. of *The Quadroone, Graham's Lady's and Gentleman's Magazine* 18 (June 1841): 296; Rev. of *The Quadroone, Ladies' Companion* 15 (May 1841): 48.

17. Letter, Ingraham to Harper & Brothers, December 10, 1839.
18. Letter, Ingraham to Fletcher Harper, January 31, 1840.

Chapter Four

1. *Charles Blackford. Or, The Adventures of a Student in Search of a Profession* (Boston: 'Yankee' Office, 1845), p. 4. Future references are parenthetical. Full citations for most novels mentioned in this chapter will be found only in the bibliography.
2. Jacob Blanck, *Bibliography of American Literature*, IV (New Haven: Yale University Press), p. 463; Arthur Herman Wilson, *A History of the Philadelphia Theatre, 1835-1855* (New York: Greenwood Press, 1968), p. 75. No copy of the play is extant.
3. David Brion Davis, *Homocide in American Fiction, 1798-1860: A Study in Social Values* (Ithaca: Cornell University Press, 1957), p. 165.
4. November 1, 1843, p. 2.
5. Letter, Ingraham to Harper & Brothers, October 8, 1841.
6. James Joseph Kinney, in his "The Theme of Miscegenation in the American Novel to World War I," Diss. University of Tennessee 1972, p. 28, points out that Ingraham established the convention of a quadroone's honor and feminine beauty in American literature.
7. Letter, Ingraham to Harper & Brothers, May 29, 1839.

Chapter Five

1. Warren Graham French, in his "Joseph Holt Ingraham, Southern Romancer, 1809-1860," Thesis. University of Texas 1948, compiled a beginning bibliography. The present writer's "Joseph Holt Ingraham: A Critical Introduction to the Man and His Works," Diss. University of Tennessee 1974, expands the listings greatly, and there are certainly more items that remain to be unearthed. Full citations for most items listed in this chapter will be found only in the bibliography.
2. *Natchez Courier: and Adams, Jefferson and Franklin Advertiser*, August 23, 1833, p. 3.
3. Winfred Gregory, *American Newspapers: 1821-1936. A Union List of Files Available in the United States and Canada* (New York: H. W. Wilson Co., 1937), p. 347.
4. "Letters from Louisiana and Mississippi By a Yankee," *Natchez Courier & Journal*, January 9, 1835, p. 1.
5. Warren G. French, "The Twice-Told Travels of Joseph Holt Ingraham," *American Notes and Queries* 1 (December 1962): 51.
6. "Extract . . . Leaf No. II," *Gentleman's Magazine* 3 (September 1838): 171.
7. Correspondence of the Natchez Courier," *Weekly Courier & Journal*, July 21, 1837, p. 2.

8. *Southern Literary Messenger* 4 (May 1838): 299.
9. *Southern Literary Messenger* 4 (June 1838): 374.
10. "Biographical Sketches of Living American Poets and Novelists. No. IV. William Gilmore Simms, Esq.," *Southern Literary Messenger* 4 (August 1838): 529, 535.
11. *Boston Miscellany of Literature and Fashion* 2 (October 1842): 187.
12. *Portland Transcript*, December 2, 1837, p. 272.
13. Letter, Ingrahame [*sic*] to George Roberts, July 10, 1841. Ms. owned by Boston Public Library and reprinted with the permission of the Trustees.
14. J. H. Ingraham, "An Evening at Buccleuch Hall; or, The Grenadier's Ghost. A Tale of the Old Stair Head Clock," *Ladies Companion* 17 (August 1842): 166-71. Future references are parenthetical.
15. "Harvey Ross; or, The Smithy of 'The Echo Road.' A Tale of a Tobacco Chewer," *Ladies' Companion* NS 1 (May 1844): 14.
16. "The Tobacco-Chewer's Temptation; or The First Lie. Being Part Second to Harvey Ross," *Ladies' Companion* NS 1 (June 1844): 60.
17. "The Judgement; or, Hope in Despair. The Sequel to the Tobacco-Chewer. A Tale for the People," *Ladies' Companion* NS 1 (August 1844): 177.
18. Letter, Ingrahame [*sic*] to Edward Carey, April 6, 1839. Ms. owned by the Historical Society of Pennsylvania and reprinted with their permission.
19 *United States Magazine, and Democratic Review* 1 (February 1838): 349. Future references are parenthetical.
20. *United States Magazine, and Democratic Review* 3 (November 1838): 248-49.
21. *West Point; or A Tale of Treason, An Historical Drama, in Three Acts* (n.p. [Baltimore: Bull and Tuttle], n.d. [1840]), p. 2.
22. *Ladies' Companion* 17 (August 1842): 219-28. Future references are parenthetical.
23. Wilber Henry Ward, "Bacon's Rebellion in Literature to 1861," Diss. University of Tennessee 1971, pp. 182, 181, 185.
24. Ibid., p. 185.
25. *Evergreen* 10 (December 1853): 435.
26. Gregory, p. 482.

Chapter Six

1. *Prince*, 2nd. ed. (1859; reprint ed., Boston: Roberts Brothers, 1897), p. xi.
2. Warren G. French, "A Hundred Years of a Religious Bestseller," *Western Humanities Review* 10 (Winter 1955-56): 49.
3. Ibid., pp. 54, 52.

4. Review of *The Pillar of Fire*, by Rev. J. H. Ingraham, *Portland Transcript*, April 30, 1859, p. 3.

5. Review of *The Pillar of Fire*, by Rev. J. H. Ingraham, *Knickerbocker* 53 (June 1859): 639.

6. Jacob Blanck, *Bibliography of American Literature*, 4 (New Haven: Yale University Press, 1963), p. 484.

7. Letter, Ingraham to Fletcher Harper. August 27, 1855.

8. Charles S. Sydnor, *A Gentleman of the Old Natchez Region: Benjamin L. C. Wailes* (Durham: Duke University Press, 1838), p. 133.

Chapter Seven

1. Portland *Eastern Argus*, March 22, 1845, p. 2.

2. Raymond L. Kilgour, *Messrs. Roberts Brothers Publishers* (Ann Arbor: University of Michigan Press, 1952), p. 20.

Selected Bibliography

PRIMARY SOURCES

1. Manuscripts

The following letters are located in the Department of Rare Books and Manuscripts of the Boston Public Library, Boston, Massachusetts:

Letter, Ingrahame [sic] to George Roberts, July 10, 1841.
Letter, Ingraham to [H. Hooker?], April 13, 1855.

The following manuscripts were located in the files of Harper & Row, New York, when the present author completed his study. They are now in the Butler Library of Columbia University:

Contract, Ingraham and Harper & Brothers, September 29, 1836.
Contract, Ingraham and Harper & Brothers, January 17, 1839.
Letter, Ingraham to Harper & Brothers, December 10, 1839.
Letter, Ingraham to Fletcher Harper, January 31, 1840.
Letter, Ingraham to Harper & Brothers, May 29, 1839.

The following manuscripts are located in the Historical Society of Pennsylvania, Philadelphia, Pennsylvania:

Letter, Ingrahame [sic] to Edward Carey, April 6, 1839.
Letter, Ingrahame [sic] to Ann S. Stephens, July 5, 1839.
Letter, Ingraham to Ketchum & Fessenden, November 7, 1843.

The following manuscripts are located in the Massachusetts Historical Society, Boston, Massachusetts:

Letter, Ingraham to Horace Mann, June 27, 1848.
Letter, Ingraham to Horace Mann, November 1, 1848.

The following manuscript is located in the National Archives, Washington, D.C.:

Letter, Ingraham to Daniel Webster, June 15, 1841.

The following manuscripts are located in the Manuscripts and Archives Division, New York Public Library, New York City:

Letter, Ingraham to J. J. Smith, November 24, 1839.
Letter, Ingraham to W. H. Butterworth, August 21, 1841.
Promissory note, Ingraham to Charles S. Rowell, August 21, 1841.

The following manuscripts are located in the Pierpont Morgan Library, New York City:

Letter, Ingraham [to Fletcher Harper?], March 17, 1857.
Letter, Ingraham [to Fletcher Harper?], March 23, 1857.
Letter, Ingraham to Fletcher Harper, April 12, 1858.

The following manuscripts are located in the Ingraham Collection, Barrett Library, University of Virginia Library, Charlottesville, Virginia:

Letter, Ingrahame [sic] to George Roberts, July 8, [1841?].
Letter, Ingraham to Mrs. Anne M. Hall, November 8, 1859.

The following manuscripts are located in the Beinecke Rare Book and Manuscript Library, Yale University, New Haven, Connecticut:

Letter, Ingraham to Rev. Jeremiah Day, June 29, 1828.
Letter, Ingraham to Rev. Jeremiah Day, February 21, 1830.

2. Periodicals, Newspapers, Gift Books, and Parish Reports

"The Assassin's Sister, or The Night Before Execution. A Sketch." *Symbol, and Odd Fellow's Magazine* 3 (August 1844):259-64.
"Biographical Sketches of Living American Poets and Novelists." "No. I. Francis William Thomas, Esq." *Southern Literary Messenger* 4 (May 1838):297-301; "No. II. James Fenimore Cooper, Esq." (June 1838):373-78; "No. III. William D. Gallagher, Esq." (July 1838):452-57; "No. IV. William Gilmore Simms, Esq." (August 1838):528-35. Reprinted from the Natchez *Weekly Courier & Journal*, where the sketches appeared as "Literary Sketches."
"The Bivouac: or, A Night at the Mouth of the Ohio. A Sketch of Western Voyaging." *Boston Miscellany of Literature and Fashion* 2 (July 1842): 40-44. Reprinted in *The Spectre Steamer, and Other Tales* (1846).
"The 'Black Knight's Ride'; or, Clare of Cleaves; A Legend of the Castle of Ehrenbreitstein." *Godey's Lady's Book* 21 (September 1840): 97-107.

"The Black Patch; or, A Year and a Day." *The American Lounger; or, Tales, Sketches, and Legends Gathered in Sundry Journeyings.* Philadelphia: Lea and Blanchard, 1839, pp. 253-73.

"The Bold Insurgent. A Tale of the Year 1675." *Ladies' Companion* 17 (August 1842), 219-28. Reprinted in *The Young Artist, and the Bold Insurgent* (1846).

"Carlota, The Nun of San Eliseo. A Tale of Louisiana. In Two Parts." *Ladies' Companion* 19 (June 1843): 58-65; "Part II." (July 1843): 110-17.

"The Dancing Star: or, The Smuggler of the Chesapeake. A Story of the Coast and Sea." *Weekly Novelette* 1 (August 8, 1857): 321-30; (August 15, 1857); 337-44; (August 22, 1857): 353-60; (August 29, 1857): 370-75.

"Dots and Lines,—No. I; Or, Sketches of Scenes and Incidents in the West." *Ladies' Companion* 11 (May 1839): 38-41; "No. II." (June 1839): 69-71; "No. III." (July 1839): 123-24; "No. IV." (August 1839): 196; "No. V." (September 1839): 243-44.

"Elfrida, The Druid's Daughter; or, The Cross Planted in Britain. A Tale of the First Century." *Churchman's Monthly Magazine* 3 (January 1856): 23-26; (February 1856): 111-16; (March 1856): 138-43; (April 1856): 222-28; (May 1856): 265-70; (June 1856): 330-36; (July 1856): 416-23; (August 1856): 467-73; (September 1856): 539-44; (October 1856): 612-18.

"An Evening at Buccleuch Hall; or, The Grenadier's Ghost. A Tale of the Old Stair Head Clock." *Ladies' Companion* 17 (July 1842): 166-71.

"Extract from the Journal of a Passenger from Philadelphia to New Orleans. Leaf. No. I." *Gentleman's Magazine* 3 (August 1838): 92-95; "Leaf No. II." (September 1838): 170-73; "Leaf No. III." (October 1838): 221-23; "Leaf No. IV." (November 1838): 305-7. Most of this material seems to have come from *The South-West* (1835).

"The General's Niece, or A Gun-Brig Adventure. A Tale of Havana." *Symbol, and Odd Fellow's Magazine* 4 (February 1845): 53-58.

"Glimpses at Gotham, Number I." *Ladies' Companion* 10 (January 1839): 110-11; "No. II." (February 1839): 177-78; "No. III." (March 1839): 229-31; "No. IV." (April 1839): 282-91.

"The Green Huntsman; or, The Haunted Villa. A Christmas Legend of Louisiana." *Ladies' Companion* 15 (June 1841): 69-74.

"Harvey Ross; or, The Smithy of 'The Echo Road.' A Tale of a Tobacco Chewer." *Ladies' Companion* 1 (May 1844): 11-17.

"Human Life." *Portland Transcript*, December 2, 1837, p. 272.

"The Judgment; or, Hope in Despair. The Sequel to the Tobacco-Chewer. A Tale for the People." *Ladies' Companion*, NS 1 (August 1844): 173-80.

"The Kennebec Sloop. And the English Cruisers." *Eastern Argus*, September 24, 1845, p. 2.

"Letters from Adina, Daughter of Manasseh, The Rich Jew of Alexandria, to Her Father. Written from Jerusalem in the Days of Pontius Pilate; Translated from the Alexandrian MSS. in the *Biblioteque Antique* of Cairo, in Egypt." *The Evergreen, A Repository of Religious, Literary and Entertaining Knowledge, for the Christian Family* 7 (August 1850): 242-47; "Letter Second" (October 1850): 307-10; "Letter Third" (November 1850): 334-37; [Letter Four was not printed in *The Evergreen* though it appears in the 1855 and 1859 editions of *The Prince of the House of David*]; "Letter Fifth" (December 1850): 354-66; "Second Series.—Letter First" 8 (January 1851): 3-7; "Second Series.—Letter Second" (February 1851): 46-50; "Second Series.—Letter Third" (March 1851): 82-86; "Second Series.—Letter Fourth" (April 1851): 116-19; "Second Series.—Letter Fifth" (May 1851): 132-35; "Second Series.—Letter Sixth" (June 1851): 170-73; "Second Series.—Letter Seventh" (July 1851): 201-204; "Second Series.—Letter Eighth" (August 1851): 228-31; "Second Series.—Letter Ninth" (September 1851): 268-71; "Second Series.—Letter Tenth" (October 1851): 301-304; "Second Series.—Letter Eleventh" (November 1851): 346-50; "Second Series.—Letter Twelfth" (December 1851): 356-60; "No. I" 9 (January 1852): 19-22; "No. II" (February 1852): 47-51; "No. III" (March 1852): 87-90; "No. IV" (April 1852): 110-13; "No. V" (May 1852): 148-52; "No. VI" (August 1852): 229-31; "No. VII" (September 1852): 268-70; "No. VIII" (October 1852): 300-303; 10 (January 1853): 5-8; (February 1853): 35-39; (March 1853): 75-79; (April 1853): 115-20; (June 1853): 202-206; (July 1853): 228-33; (September 1853): 309-14; (October 1853): 340-44; (November 1853): 381-85; (December 1853): 415-35.

"Letters from Louisiana and Mississippi. By a Yankee.—Number I." *Natchez Courier: and Adams, Jefferson and Franklin Advertiser*, August 23, 1833, p. 3; "Number II," September 6, 1833, p. 3; "Number III," September 13, 1833 [entry postulated, pp. 3-4 are missing]; "Number IV," September 20, 1833, pp. 2-3; "Number V," October 4, 1833, p. 3; "Number VI," October 11, 1833, p. 3; "Number VII," October 18, 1833, p. 3; "Number VIII," October 25, 1833, p. 3; "Number IX," November 1, 1833, pp. 2-3; "Number X," December 6, 1833, p. 1; "Number XI," December 20, 1833, p.

"Letters from Louisiana and Mississippi By a Yankee. Second Series.— "Number VI," Natchez *Courier & Journal*, January 2, 1835, p. 1; "Number VII," January 9, 1835, p. 1; "Number VIII," January 16, 1835, p. 1.

Selected Bibliography

"Lines to the Bunker-Hill Monument." *Boston Miscellany of Literature and Fashion* 2 (October 1842): 187.
"The Lottery Ticket." *Ladies' Companion* 18 (April 1843): 273-79. Reprinted in *The Spectre Steamer, and Other Tales* (1846).
"The Midnight Guest." *Ballou's Pictorial Drawing-Room Companion* 8 (June 2, 1855): 342-43.
"Mississippi. Aberdeen." *Spirit of Missions* 16 (September 1851): 409-10; (December 1851): 504.
"Mississippi. Aberdeen." *Spirit of Missions* 17 (May 1852): 143-44.
"Mississippi. Aberdeen." Spirit of Missions 18 (April 1853): 97; (May 1853): 132-34.
"Mississippi. Aberdeen." *Spirit of Missions* 19 (1854): 119.
"Mrs. Nicholas Muggs; or, The Hoax." *The Gift: A Christmas and New Year's Present for 1839*, ed. Miss Leslie. Philadelphia: E. L. Carey & A. Hart, [1838], pp. 110-44.
"Mysteries in My Parish: or, The Pencilled Fly-Leaves from the Private Diary of a Clergyman." *Churchman's Monthly Magazine* 1 (August 1854): 466-71; "No. II." (September 1854): 529-34; "The Two Graves." (November 1854): 685-88, 673-74; "No. III." (December 1854): 730-36.
"The Old Mansion." *Ladies' Companion* 20 (December 1842): 70-72.
"The Poet's Curse; or, 'We Shall Be Rich To-Morrow.'" *Ladies' Companion*, NS 1 (September 1844): 244-47.
"The Quadroon of Orleans. A Tale." *The American Lounger: or, Tales, Sketches, and Legends Gathered in Sundry Journeyings.* Philadelphia: Lea and Blanchard, 1839, pp. 253-73.
"The Raritan." *American Melodies*, ed. George P. Morris, pp. 130-31. New York: Linen and Fennell, [1841].
[Report] *Journal of the Proceedings of the Twenty-Sixth Annual Convention of the Protestant Episcopal Church, in the Diocese of Alabama.* Mobile: Farrow & Dennett, 1857, p. 11.
[Report on the Tennessee Penitentiary]. *Journal of the Proceedings of the Twenty-Second Annual Convention of the Clergy and Laity of the Protestant Episcopal Church, in the Diocese of Tennessee.* Columbia: Mitchell & Rainey, 1850, pp. 23-24.
"The Robber in 'Boots'; or, The Midnight Alarm.—Being an Account of Mr. Varian Wallace Wells' First Visit to the City." *Ladies' Companion* 20 (February 1844): 182-88, 203-204.
"[Romance of American History. No. I.] The Charter, An Historical Tale of Connecticut," *United States Magazine, and Democratic Review* 1 (February 1838): 330-54. "No. II. West Point,—A Tale of Treason" 3 (November 1838): 235-51; (December 1838); 339-56. "West Point" was reprinted as "Arnold; or the British Spy. A Tale of Treachery and Treason," *Ladies' Companion* 17 (May 1842): 57-65; (June 1842): 76-82, and as *Arnold: or The British Spy! A*

Tale of Treason and Treachery (Boston: 'Yankee' Office, 1844), and as *The Treason of Arnold. A Tale of West Point. During the American Revolution* (Jonesville, Mass.: James M. Barnes, 1847). Joseph Breck dramatized Ingraham's tale as *West Point; or A Tale of Treason, An Historical Drama, in Three Acts*. Baltimore: Bull and Tuttle, [1840]. "No. III. The Hostile Governors." 6 (November 1839): 399-411. This story reappeared as part of chapter one of *The Quadroone* (1841).

"The Sacred Fire." *The Token and Atlantic Souvenir, A Christmas and New Year's Present*. Boston: Otis, Broaders, and Co., 1838, pp. 242-80.

"St. John's Church, Aberdeen; St. Paul's Church, Columbus." *Journal of the Proceedings of the Twenty-Fifth Annual Convention of the Protestant Episcopal Church, in the Diocese of Mississippi*. Natchez: Natchez Courier Book and Job Office, 1851, pp. 43-44.

"St. John's Church, Aberdeen." *Diocese of Mississippi. Twenty-Seventh Annual Convention*. n.p., [1853], pp. 68-69.

"St. John's Church, Mobile." *Journal of the Proceedings of the Twenty-Third Annual Convention of the Protestant Episcopal Church, in the Diocese of Alabama*. Mobile: Benjamin, Farrow & Co., 1854, p. 17.

"St. John's Church, Mobile." *Journal of the Proceedings of the Twenty-Fourth Annual Convention of the Protestant Episcopal Church, in the Diocese of Alabama*. Mobile: Farrow, Stokes & Dennett, 1855, pp. 14-15.

"St. John's Church, Mobile." *Journal of the Proceedings of the Twenty-Fifth Annual Convention of the Protestant Episcopal Church, in the Diocese of Alabama*. Mobile: Farrow, Stokes & Dennett, 1856, p. 15.

"Secrets of the Cells: or Leaves From My Diary." *Ballou's Pictorial Drawing-Room Companion* 8 (March 7, 1855): 162-64; (March 24, 1855): 178-79; (March 31, 1855): 194-95; (April 7, 1855): 210-11; (April 14, 1855): 226-27; (April 21, 1855): 242-43. Jacob Blanck lists "Secrets of the Cells" as an unlocated title in his *Bibliography of American Literature*, IV (New Haven: Yale University Press, 1963), p. 489. There is no evidence to suggest that "Secrets" was ever published in book form. Serials in *Ballou's* that were reprinted were extensively advertised in the periodical, and "Secrets" was not mentioned again after its initial publication.

"Sketches in the West. No. I." *Ladies' Companion* 13 (June 1840): 67-68; "No. II." (July 1840): 139-40; "No. III." (August 1840): 202-203; "No. IV" (September 1840): 215-16; "No. V." (October 1840): 281-82; "No. VI." (December 1840): 91-92; "No. VII." (January 1841): 127-28; "No. VIII." (February 1841): 281-82.

"The Spectre Steamer; or, Hugh Northup's Oath. A Tale of the Mississippi." *Ladies' Companion* 15 (September 1841): 231-36.

Selected Bibliography

Reprinted in *The Spectre Steamer, and Other Tales* (1846).
"Spheeksphobia: or, The Adventures of Abel Stingflyer, A. M. A Tragic Tale," *Southern Literary Messenger* 3 (October 1837): 585-93. Reprinted in *The American Lounger* (1839).
"Tales of the Knights of Seven Lands; A Series of Romanceros of Chivalry. Tale the First; Being the Story of Don Fernando De Valor." *Boston Miscellany of Literature and Fashion* 2 (September 1842): 126-32; "The Story of the Sieur Louis De Linant" (October 1842): 145-51; "The Story of the Sieur Louis De Linant, Concluded. Showing How the Princess Beatriz Avenged Herself for the Treachery of the Count Alarcos" (November 1842): 199-205; "The Tale of Rother De Ernest, the German Knight" (December 1842): 254-59; "The Story of Pier Farnese, the Venetian Knight" 3 (January 1843): 38-41. The "Pier Farnese" tale is incomplete, and the rest of the series was not published here because the periodical ceased publication. These four tales, with the addition of two others, were published as *The Knights of Seven Lands* (1845). The title is misleading, for the published volume contained only six tales.
"The Tobacco-Chewer's Temptation; or, The First Lie. Being Part Second to Harvey Ross." *Ladies' Companion*, NS 1 (June 1844): 59-64.
"Travelling for Pleasure." *Ladies' Companion* 13 (January 1840): 148.
"The Village Prize." *Portland Sketch Book*, ed. Ann S. Stephens. Portland, Maine: Colman and Chisholm, 1836, pp. 126-34. Reprinted in *The American Lounger* (1839) as "The Mysterious Leaper; or, The Courtship of Mine Host's Daughter."
"The Young Artist. A Story. Suggested by Mount's Picture of 'The Painter's Study,' in the Possession of Edward L. Carey, Esq. Part First." *Godey's Lady's Book* 20 (February 1840): 81-85; (March 1840): 113-19. Reprinted in 1846 in *The Young Artist, and the Bold Insurgent*.

3. Novels and Other Works

Alice May, and Bruising Bill. Boston: Gleason's Publishing Hall, 1845.
The American Lounger; or, Tales, Sketches, and Legends Gathered in Sundry Journeyings. Philadelphia: Lea & Blanchard, 1839.
Arnold: or the British Spy! A Tale of Treason and Treachery. Boston: 'Yankee' Office, 1844. "The Bold Insurgent" is also reprinted.
Arthur Denwood: or The Maiden of the Inn. A Tale of the War of 1812. Boston: H. L. Williams, 1846.
Beatrice, the Goldsmith's Daughter. [A St]ory of the Reign of the Last Charles. Boston: Williams Brothers, 1847. "Duncan Campbell" is also included.

The Beautiful Unknown; or, Massey Finke. Boston: 'Yankee' Office, 1844. Jacob Blanck's *Bibliography of American Literature,* IV (New Haven: Yale University Press, 1963), p. 489, lists the title as unlocated. The novel has been microfilmed and appears in the Lyle H. Wright *American Fiction* series.

Berkeley: or, the Lost and Redeemed. A Novel. Boston: Henry L. Williams, 1846.

Bertrand, or, The Story of Marie De Heywode. Being a Sequel to Marie, the Fugitive. Boston: H. L. Williams, 1845.

Biddy Woodhull; or The Pretty Haymaker. Boston: E. P. Williams, 1844.

The Bold Insurgent. A Tale of the Year 1768. Boston: 'Yankee' Office, 1844.

Bonfield; or, The Outlaw of the Bermudas. A Nautical Novel. Boston: H. L. Williams, 1846.

La Bonita Cigarera; or The Beautiful Cigar Vender. A Tale of New York. Boston: 'Yankee' Office, 1844.

Burton: or The Sieges. A Romance. 2 vols. New York: Harper & Brothers, 1838.

Captain Kyd; or, The Wizard of the Sea. A Romance. 2 vols. New York: Harper & Brothers, 1839.

Caroline Archer; or, The Miliner's [sic] Apprentice. A Story that Hath More Truth than Fiction in It. Boston: Edward P. Williams, [1844]. Also reprints "The Pretty Feet: or, The Way to Choose a Wife" and "The Gaiter Boots. A Sequel to the Story of 'The Pretty Feet.'"

Charles Blackford. Or, the Adventures of a Student in Search of a Profession. Boston: 'Yankee' Office, 1845.

The Clipper-Yacht; or, Moloch, the Money-Lender! A Tale of London, and the Thames. Boston: H. L. Williams, 1845.

The Corsair of Casco Bay or The Pilot's Daughter. Gardiner, Maine: G. M. Atwood, 1844.

The Dancing Feather; or, The Amateur Freebooters. A Romance of New York. [Boston: George Roberts], [1842].

Edward Austin: or, The Hunting Flask. A Tale of the Forest and Town. Boston: F. Gleason, 1842.

Eleanor Sherwood, the Beautiful Temptress! [Boston: 'Yankee' Office], [1843].

Estelle: or, The Conspirator of the Isle. A Tale of the West Indian Seas. Boston: 'Yankee' Office, 1844.

Fleming Field; or The Young Artisan. A Tale of the Days of the Stamp Act. New York: Burgess, Stringer and Co., 1845.

Forrestal: or The Light of the Reef. A Romance of the Blue Waters. Boston: H. L. Williams (Yankee Office), 1845.

Frank Rivers: or, The Dangers of the Town. [Boston: E. P. Williams], [1843].

Freemantle: or, The Privateersman! A Nautical Romance of the Last War. Boston: George W. Redding and Co., 1845.
The Free-Trader; or, The Cruiser of Narragansett Bay. New York: Williams Brothers, 1847.
The Gipsy of the Highlands or, The Jew and the Heir. Being the Adventures of Duncan Powell and Paul Tatnall. Boston: Redding & Co., 1843.
Grace Weldon; or, Frederica, the Bonnet Girl. A Tale of Boston and its Bay. Boston: Williams, 1845.
Harry Harefoot. [Boston: 'Yankee' Office], [1845].
Herman DeRuyter; or, The Mystery Unveiled. A Sequel to the Beautiful Cigar Vender. A Tale of the Metropolis. Boston: 'Yankee' Office, 1844.
Howard: or, The Mysterious Disappearance. [Boston: Edward P. Williams], [1843].
Jemmy Daily: or, The Little News Vender. A Tale of Youthful Struggles, and the Triumph of Truth and Virtue over Vice and Falsehood. Boston: Brainard and Co., 1843.
The Lady of the Gulf. A Romance of the City and the Seas. Boston: H. L. Williams, 1846.
Lafitte: the Pirate of the Gulf. 1836; reprint ed., Upper Saddle River, N.J.: Gregg Press, 1970.
Leisler: or The Rebel and King's Man. A Tale of the Rebellion of 1689. Boston: Henry L. Williams, 1846.
Marie; or, The Fugitive. A Romance of Mount Benedict. Boston: 'Yankee' Office, 1845.
Mary Wilbur: or, The Deacon and the Widow's Daughter. Boston: 'Yankee' Office, [1845].
The Mast-Ship: or, The Bombardment of Falmouth. Boston: Henry L. Williams, 1845.
Mate Burke; or, The Foundlings of the Sea. New York: Burgess, Stringer and Co., 1846.
The Midshipman, or The Corvette and Brigantine. A Tale of Sea and Land. Boston: F. Gleason, 1844.
The Miseries of New York. Or the Burglar and Counsellor. Boston: 'Yankee' Office, 1844.
Montezuma, the Serf, or The Revolt of the Mexitili. A Tale of the Last Days of the Aztec Dynasty. 2 vols. Boston: H. L. Williams, 1845.
Morris Graeme: or, The Cruise of the Sea-Slipper. A Sequel to the Dancing Feather. A Tale of the Land and the Sea. Boston: E. P. Williams, 1843.
Neal Nelson. [Boston: Williams], [1845].
Norman: or, The Privateersman's Bride. A Sequel to "Freemantle." Boston: H. L. Williams, 1845.
The Odd Fellow, or, The Secret Association, and Foraging Peter.

Boston: United States Publishing Co., 1846.
Pamphlets for the People. In Illustration of the Claims of the Church and Methodism. Philadelphia: H. Hooker, 1854.
Paul Deverell, or Two Judgments for One Crime: A Tale of the Present Day. Boston: H. L. Williams, 1845.
Paul Perril, the Merchant's Son: or The Adventures of a New-England Boy Launched Upon Life. 2 vols. Boston: Williams and Brothers, [1847].
Pierce Fenning, or, The Lugger's Chase. A Romance. Boston: Henry L. Williams, 1846.
The Pillar of Fire; or, Israel in Bondage. 1859; reprint ed., Boston: Roberts Brothers, 1882.
The Prince of the House of David; or Three Years in the Holy City. Being a Series of the Letters of Adina, a Jewess of Alexandria, Sojourning in Jerusalem in the Days of Herod, Addressed to Her Father, a Wealthy Jew in Egypt, and Relating, as by an Eye-Witness, All the Scenes and Wonderful Incidents in the Life of Jesus of Nazareth, from His Baptism in Jordan to His Crucifixion on Calvary. New York: Pudney & Russell, 1855.
The Prince of the House of David; or, Three Years in the Holy City. Being a Series of the Letters of Adina, A Jewess of Alexandria, Supposed to be Sojourning in Jerusalem in the Days of Herod, Addressed to Her Father, a Wealthy Jew in Egypt, and Relating, as if by an Eye-Witness, All the Scenes and Wonderful Incidents in the Life of Jesus of Nazareth, from His Baptism in Jordan to His Crucifixion on Calvary. 2d ed. 1859; reprint ed., Boston: Roberts Brothers, 1897.
The Quadroone; or St. Michael's Day. 2 vols. New York: Harper & Brothers, 1841.
Rafael: or, The Twice Condemned. A Tale of Key West. Boston: H. L. Williams, 1845.
Report Upon a Proposed System of Public Education, for the City of Nashville, Respectfully Addressed to its Citizens. Nashville: W. F. Bang & Co., 1848.
The Ringdove: or, The Privateer and the Cutter. Boston: H. L. Williams, 1846. Jacob Blanck's *Bibliography of American Literature*, IV (New Haven: Yale University Press, 1963), p. 478, lists *The Ringdove* as not located. A copy is in the Mississippi State Department of Archives and History.
Santa Claus: or, The Merry King of Christmas. Boston: H. L. Williams, 1844.
Scarlet Feather, or The Young Chief of the Abenaquies. A Romance of the Wilderness of Maine. Boston: F. Gleason, 1845.
The Slave King; or The Triumph of Liberty. 2 vols. Boston: H. L. Williams, 1846.

The South-West. 2 vols. 1835; reprint ed., Ann Arbor: University Microfilms, Inc., 1966.
The Spanish Galleon; or The Pirate of the Mediterranean. A Romance of the Corsair Kidd. Boston: F. Gleason, 1845.
Steel Belt: or, The Three Masted Goleta! A Tale of Boston Bay. Boston: 'Yankee' Office, 1844.
The Sunny South; or, The Southerner at Home, Embracing Five Years' Experience of a Northern Governess in the Land of the Sugar and the Cotton. 1860; reprint ed., New York: Negro Universities Press, 1968.
The Surf Skiff: or, The Heroine of the Kennebec. Boston: Williams Brothers, 1847. "Captain Velasco; and the Young Lieutenant. Or, Our Private Bucanneering Adventure" also appears in this volume.
Theodore; or, The 'Child of the Sea.' Being a Sequel to the Novel of "Lafitte, the Pirate of the Gulf." Boston: Edward P. Williams, 1844.
The Throne of David; from the Consecration of the Shepherd of Bethlehem, to the Rebellion of Prince Absalom. Being an Illustration of the Splendor, Power, and Dominion of the Reign of the Shepherd, —Poet, —Warrior, —King, and Prophet, Ancestor and Type of Jesus; in a Series of Letters Addressed by an Assyrian Ambassador, Resident at the Court of Saul and David, to his Lord and King on the Throne of Nineveh; Wherein the Glory of Assyria, as well as the Magnificence of Judea, is Presented to the Reader as by an Eye Witness. Philadelphia: G. G. Evans, 1860.
The Young Artist, and the Bold Insurgent. Boston: United States Publishing Co., 1846.
The Young Genius; or, Trials and Triumphs. Boston: E. P. Williams, 1843.

SECONDARY SOURCES

AUNT ROSIE [MRS. S. L. FALCONER]. "Last Days of the Rev. Dr. Ingraham." Typescript, Kate Freeman Clark Museum, Holly Springs, Mississippi. Possibly a newspaper account of Ingraham's last days.
Biographical Memoranda Respecting All Who Ever Were Members of the Class of 1832 in Yale College. New Haven: Yale University, 1880. Brief, occasionally untrustworthy, comments on Ingraham.
BISHOP, DAVID H. "Joseph Holt Ingraham." In *Library of Southern Literature,* VI, ed. Edwin Anderson Alderman and Joel Chandler Harris. New Orleans: The Martin and Hoyt Company, 1907, pp. 2591-96. Untrustworthy biographical information and some excerpts from Ingraham's works.
BLANCK, JACOB. *Bibliography of American Literature,* IV. New Haven: Yale University Press, 1963, pp. 459-91. Most complete listing of

hardbound and paperbound novels.

COWIE, ALEXANDER. *The Rise of the American Novel.* New York: American Book Co., 1948. Contains an analysis of *Lafitte.*

DONDORE, DOROTHY ANNE. "Joseph Holt Ingraham." In *Dictionary of American Biography,* IX. New York: Charles Scribner's Sons, 1932, 479-80. Occasionally untrustworthy biography.

EXMAN, EUGENE. *The Brothers Harper. A Unique Publishing Partnership and Its Impact Upon the Cultural Life of America from 1817 to 1853.* New York: Harper & Row, 1965. Brief mention of Ingraham's work for the firm.

FRENCH, WARREN G. "A Hundred Years of a Religious Bestseller," *Western Humanities Review* 10 (Winter 1955-1956): 45-54. Study of *Prince.*

———. "Joseph Holt Ingraham, Southern Romancer, 1809-1860." University of Texas M.A. Thesis, 1948. The first modern scholarly study of Ingraham.

———. "A Sketch of the Life of Joseph Holt Ingraham." *The Journal of Mississippi History* 11 (July 1949): 155-71. Good, though now superseded, study based on the above thesis.

———. "The Twice-Told Travels of Joseph Holt Ingraham." *American Notes and Queries* 1 (December 1962): 51-52. On the relationship between *The South-West* (1835) and "Extracts from the Journal of a Passenger from Philadelphia to New Orleans" (1838).

HART, JAMES D. *The Popular Book: A History of America's Literary Taste.* Los Angeles: University of California Press, 1961. A study of popular reading tastes.

HUBBELL, JAY B. *The South in American Literature: 1607-1900.* Durham: Duke University Press, 1954. Good brief biography with bibliography.

INGRAHAM, LANGLEY. "Memoirs of Rev. J. H. Ingraham." Typescript, May 23, 1930, Maine Historical Society. Notes by a grandson who never knew the author. Untrustworthy on some points.

JOHANNSEN, ALBERT. *The House of Beadle and Adams and Its Dime and Nickel Novels. The Story of a Vanished Literature,* II. Norman: University of Oklahoma Press, 1950. Good brief biographical sketch with one of two known pictures of Ingraham.

KILGOUR, RAYMOND L. *Messrs. Roberts Brothers Publishers.* Ann Arbor: University of Michigan Press, 1952. Comments on the religious novels and their sales.

MACBLAIN, REV. RAYMOND E. *Christ Church. Its History and Tradition.* n.p. [Holly Spring, Miss.], 1936. History of Christ Church with some erroneous information on Ingraham.

MOTT, FRANK LUTHER. *Golden Multitudes: The Story of Best Sellers in the United States.* New York: R. R. Bowker Co., 1947. A study of best-sellers with estimates of their sales.

Selected Bibliography

NELSON, LUCY GREEN. *St. John's Church, Mobile. A History.* Mobile: Jordan Printing Co., 1963. History of St. John's with appreciative sketch of Ingraham's life.

PENNINGTON, EDGAR LEGARE. "The Ministry of Joseph Holt Ingraham in Mobile, Alabama." *Historical Magazine of the Protestant Episcopal Church* 26 (December 1957): 344-60. Good history of Ingraham's work in Mobile.

SEITZ, DON C. "A Prince of Best Sellers." *Publisher's Weekly* 119 (February 21, 1931): 940. Gives unsubstantiated sales figures for *Prince*.

STIETENROTH, CHAS. *One Hundred Years with "Old Trinity" Church: Natchez, Miss.* Natchez: Natchez Printing & Stationery Co., 1922. Brief comments on Ingraham.

SYDNOR, CHARLES S. *A Gentleman of the Old Natchez Region: Benjamin L. C. Wailes.* Durham: Duke University Press, 1938. Account of Ingraham's relationship with Wailes.

SYKES, JAMES LUNDY. *History of Saint John's Parish: Aberdeen, Mississippi.* Aberdeen, Miss., n.d. Chronicles Ingraham's work at Aberdeen.

TURNIPSEED, JAMES OLIVER. "Joseph Holt Ingrahame, His Life and Works." M.A. thesis, Alabama Polytechnic Institute, 1938. Interesting but substantially undocumented study.

WEATHERSBY, ROBERT W., II. "J. H. Ingraham and Tennessee: A Record of Social and Literary Contributions," *Tennessee* Historical Quarterly, 34 (Fall, 1975), 264-72. Good history of Ingraham's work in Tennessee.

———. "Joseph Holt Ingraham: A Critical Introduction to the Man and His Works." Ph.D. dissertation, University of Tennessee, 1974. Superseded by the present study though still valuable for its bibliography which includes periodical material that Blanck omits.

Index

Aberdeen, Mississippi, 38, 39, 40, 43, 44
Aberdeen *Monroe Democrat*, 40
Aguilar, Grace *(Home Influence)*, 82
Alger, Horatio, 133
Arnold, Benedict, 59, 90, 107, 108
Aunt Rosie (Mrs. S. L. Falconer), 47, 48

Baltimore, Maryland, 42
Bath, Maine, 31
Ben Bruce: Scenes in the Life of a Bowery Newsboy, 84
Bentley, Richard, 27
Boston, Massachusetts, 23, 28, 31, 71
Boston Miscellany, 100
Boston Notion, 27, 28, 29
Boston *Uncle Sam*, 92
Breck, Joseph, 107-108
Brown, Charles Brockden *(Wieland)*, 82
Brown, William Hill *(The Power of Sympathy)*, 82
Buccleuch, New Jersey, 25
Buenos Aires, Argentina, 16
Burr, Aaron, 22, 58, 60
Byron, Lord, 54; Byronic hero-villain, 21, 53, 56, 58, 64, 66, 68

Carey, Edward, 24, 106
Carleton, George, 47
Churchman, 42
Churchman's Monthly Magazine, 110
Clemens, Samuel, 94
Collins (publishers), 119
Columbus, Mississippi, 38, 39
Cooper, James Fenimore, 50, 90, 91, 99

Dartmouth College, 17-18
Day, Reverend Jeremiah, 16-18, 19
DeMille, Cecil B., 45

Democratic Review, 25, 107
"Dime Novels," 82

Emerson, Ralph Waldo ("Nature"), 131
Evans, George G., 127
Evergreen, The, 38, 109

Flint, Timothy *(Recollections of the Last Ten Years)*, 20
Fort Loudon (Tennessee), 43

Gentleman's Magazine, 94
Gift, The, 106
Godey's Lady's Book, 24, 25, 82, 100, 106
Goldsmith, Oliver ("The Deserted Village"), 101
Graham's Magazine, 26, 69
Green, Bishop William Mercer, 38, 39, 42, 45, 48

Hallowell Academy, 16
Hallowell, Maine, 16
Hanover, New Hampshire, 17
Harper & Brothers, 20, 21, 22, 23, 24, 25, 27, 43, 49-70, 74, 85
Harper, Fletcher, 43, 69, 128
Harper, James, 21
Harper's New Monthly Magazine, 43, 70
Hawthorne, Nathaniel, 82, 133
Holly Springs, Mississippi, 45, 46, 47, 123

Ingraham, Benjamin J., 24, 137n51
Ingraham, Edward, 15
Ingraham, Elizabeth Thurston, 15-16
Ingraham, James Milk, 15-16
Ingraham, John Philip Thurston, 33, 37-38, 139n2
Ingraham, Joseph Holt, Jr.,

160

autobiographical elements in work, 16, 129; bankruptcy, 29-30, 32; birth, 15; church architect and builder, 40; confirmation into Episcopal Church, 33, 139n2; death, 47-48, 142n75, 143n76; family, 27, 30, 31, 137n55; first publication, 19-20, 50; marriage, 19; minister, 18, 33-48; ordination, 38, 39-40; parents, 15-16; payments for works, 20, 21, 22, 23, 24, 25, 29, 31, 32, 42-43, 50, 61, 65, 69-70, 87, 91, 133, 141n48; schooling, 16-18, 46; sermons, 44-45; teacher, 18, 34, 41, 43, 45; travels, 16, 18, 21, 23, 24, 25, 26-27, 28, 29, 31, 34, 38-39, 41, 43, 44, 45, 46, 47, 86; work with Tennessee State Penitentiary, 36-38, 140n18

FICTION DRAMATIZED
Captain Kyd, 23, 65
Dancing Feather, The, 31
Lafitte, 21, 58
"West Point," 107, 108

NOVELS,
Alice May, 88
Arnold, 30
Arthur Denwood, 87
Beatrice, 91
Beautiful Unknown, The, 89-90
Berkeley, 73, 78
Bertrand, 88
Biddy Woodhull, 73, 78
Bonfield, 85
Burton, 22, 23, 58-61, 64, 70, 87
Captain Kyd, 23, 61-65, 69, 76, 77
Caroline Archer, 90
Charles Blackford, 81-82, 134
Clipper-Yacht, The, 84-85
Corsair of Casco Bay, The, 77
Dancing Feather, The, 28, 29, 30, 31, 71, 73, 74-75, 91
Edward Austin, 77-78, 81
Eleanor Sherwood, 73, 78-79
Estelle, 85
Fleming Field, 87
Forrestal, 85
Frank Rivers, 30, 79-80, 91, 133

Freemantle, 87
Free Trader, The, 86
Gipsy of the Highlands, The, 73-74
Grace Weldon, 83
Harry Harefoot, 78
Herman DeRuyter, 30, 79, 111
Howard, 76
Jemmy Daily, 83, 84
Knights of Seven Lands, The, 100
La Bonita Cigarera, 79, 91, 111
Lady of the Gulf, The, 77
Lafitte, 21, 23, 39, 41, 53-58, 61, 64, 65, 70, 75, 77, 133
Leisler, 74, 86
Marie, 88
Mark Manly, 86
Mary Wilbur, 88-89
Mast-Ship, The, 86
Mate Burke, 82
Midshipman, The, 76, 91
Miseries of New York, The, 133
Montezuma, 85
Morris Graeme, 30, 71, 75
Neal Nelson, 87, 134
Norman, 87
Odd Fellow, The, 105
Paul Deverell, 80
Paul Perril, 16, 85, 94
Pierce Fenning, 86
Pillar of Fire, The, 45, 46, 120-123, 125
Prince of the House of David, The, 38, 42, 43, 45, 46, 109-110, 113-120, 122, 125
Quadroone, The, 24, 25, 65-70, 87, 96
Rafael, 72
Ringdove, The, 76
St. Paul, the Roman Citizen, 47, 117, 131
Santa Claus, 31
Scarlet Feather, 90-91
Serf, The, 27, 85
Slave King, The, 85
Spanish Galleon, The, 76
Steel Belt, 77
Surf Skiff, The, 74
Theodore, 75
Throne of David, The, 46, 123-127
Young Genius, The, 84

NON-FICTIONAL PROSE
"Biographical Sketches of Living American Poets and Novelists," 98-100
Pamphlets for the People, 42
Report Upon a Proposed System of Public Education, for the City of Nashville, 34-35
"Romance of Astronomy, The," 43

POETRY
"Human Life," 101-102
"Lines to the Bunker-Hill Monument," 101
"Old Mansion, The," 101
"Raritan, The," 101

SHORT STORIES
American Lounger, The, (short story collection), 24
"Arnold; or, the British Spy," 107-108
"Assassin's Sister, The," 96
"Bivouac, The," 95, 96
" 'Black Knight's Ride,' The," 100
"Black Patch, The," 96
"Bold Insurgent, The," 108-109, 111
"Carlota, the Nun of San Eliseo," 96
"Charter, The," 106-107
"Dancing Star, The," 98
"Elfrida, the Druid's Daughter," 47, 110
"Evening at Buccleuch Hall, An," 102-103, 112
"General's Niece, The," 98
"Green Huntsman, The," 103-104
"Harvey Ross," 104-105
"Kennebec Sloop, The," 98
"Legend of the Mountain of the Burning Stone, A," 85
"Letters from Adina," 109-110
"Lottery Ticket, The," 104
"Midnight Guest, The," 110
"Mrs. Nicholas Muggs," 97, 112
"Mysteries in My Parish," 111
"Poet's Curse, The," 102
"Quadroon of Orleans, The," 96, 112

"Robber in Boots, The," 97
"Romance of American History," 106
"Romance of Palenque, A," 27
"Sacred Fire, The," 95-96
"Secrets of the Cells," 110
"Sketches from the Notebook of a Parish Clergyman," 111
"Spectre Steamer, The," 95, 96
"Spheeksphobia," 19
"Tales of the Knights of Seven Lands," 100
"Village Prize, The," 21
"West Point," 87, 107-108, 111, 112, 133
"Young Artist, The," 106, 111

TRAVEL NARRATIVES
"Correspondence of the Natchez Courier," 93-94
"Dots and Lines," 94
"Extracts from the Journal of a Passenger from Philadelphia to New Orleans," 94
"Glimpses at Gotham," 95
"Letters from Louisiana and Mississippi By a Yankee," 19, 93, 94, 96
"Sketches in the West," 94
South-West, The, 19-21, 42, 50-53, 70, 93-94, 96, 128, 130, 131
Sunny South, The, 19, 42, 46, 127-131

Ingraham, Joseph Holt, Sr., 15
Ingraham, Lydia Holt, 15
Ingraham, Mary Elizabeth Odlin Brookes, 19, 48
Ingraham, Prentiss, 47, 48, 137n55
Irving, Washington, 50

Jackson, Mississippi, 39
Jefferson College, 18-19, 22, 34, 135n17, 136n18
Jewett, Helen, 79
Jones, Joseph Stevens, 23, 65

Keats, John, 134
Kennedy, John Pendleton (*Horse-Shoe Robinson*), 20; (*Rob of the Bowl*), 22

Index

Kentucky Tragedy, 79
Ketchum and Fessenden, 29-30, 183n72
Knoxville, Tennessee, 43, 44

Ladies' Companion, 23, 25, 69, 82, 94, 95, 102, 105, 107, 108
Lafitte, Jean, 53
Lea and Blanchard, 24
London, England, 38, 46, 65
Longfellow, Henry Wadsworth, 21, 22, 23, 32
Longstreet, Augustus Baldwin (*Georgia Scenes*), 20

Mann, Horace, 35-36
Medina, Louisa, 21, 58
Melville, Herman, 132
Mobile, Alabama, 39, 41, 43
Montevideo, Uruguay, 16
Mowatt, Anna Cora, 112

Nashville Daily Gazette, 37
Nashville, Tennessee, 34-38, 40, 110
Nashville Whig, 35
Natchez, The, 19
Natchez Courier: and Adams, Jefferson and Franklin Advertiser, 19, 93
Natchez *Courier and Journal*, 19, 93
Natchez Daily Courier, 44
Natchez, Mississippi, 18, 20, 23, 24, 34, 41, 44
Natchez *Mississippi Free Trader*, 39, 80
Natchez Weekly Courier, 44
Natchez *Weekly Courier & Journal*, 93, 98
Neal, John, 22
New Brunswick, New Jersey, 24
New Orleans, Louisiana, 18, 39, 52, 53, 54-55, 66, 93
New York, New York, 21, 23, 24, 25, 27, 31, 47, 49, 113
New York *Weekly Yankee*, 111

Okolona, Mississippi, 38, 39, 40, 110
Otey, Bishop James Hervey, 37, 44, 48, 139n5

Philadelphia, Pennsylvania, 21, 24, 25, 31
Philadelphia *Saturday Courier*, 42, 46, 127
Poe, Edgar Allan, 21, 25-26, 53, 57, 69, 132, 133; "Berenice," 20; "Morella," 20; "The Mystery of Marie Roget," 79; *The Narrative of Arthur Gordon Pym*, 22
Pontotoc, Mississippi, 39, 40
Portland *Eastern Argus*, 31
Portland Gazette, and Maine Advertiser, 15
Portland, Maine, 15, 16, 17, 21, 51
Portland Sketch-Book, The, 22, 25
Portland Transcript, 22
Pudney & Russell, 38, 113

Richardson, Samuel (*Pamela*), 82
Riverside, Tennessee, 43
Roberts Brothers (publishers), 133
Roberts, George, 27, 29, 102
Rogers, Mary, 79
Rose Cottage, 19, 34
Rowson, Susanna (*Charlotte Temple*), 82

Scott, Sir Walter, 57, 99, 101; *Rokeby*, 53
Sedgwick, Catharine Maria, 112
Sheldon, Charles (*In His Steps*), 113
Sigourney, Lydia, 112
Simms, William Gilmore, 28, 99, 133; *Beauchampe: or, the Kentucky Tragedy*, 79; *The Fall of the Goth*, 99; *Mellichampe*, 99; *The Partisan*, 20; *The Yemassee*, 20
Smith, Seba, 112
Sorrows of Werter, The (Goethe), 61
Southern Literary Messenger, 20, 21, 25, 53, 57, 85, 98
Southworth, E. D. E. N. (*Retribution*), 82
Stephens, Ann A., 25
Stowe, Harriet Beecher, 128
Symbol, and Odd Fellow's Magazine, 105-106

Ten Commandments, The, 46

Thomas, Francis William, 99

Uncle Tom's Cabin, 128
United States Magazine, and Democratic Review, 65-66, 105, 106
University of Mississippi, 46

Vonore, Tennessee, 43

Wailes, Benjamin L. C., 19, 20, 47
Wallace, Lew *(Ben-Hur),* 113
Ware, William *(Julian),* 113

Washington, D. C., 26
Washington, George, 22, 59
Washington, Mississippi, 18, 19, 47
Webster, Daniel, 26-27, 29
West Point, New York, 24
Whitman, Walt *(Leaves of Grass),* 42
Williams Brothers, 27, 29, 71, 133
Willis, Nathaniel P., 22, 24, 112
Wordsworth, William, 101

Yale College, 16-18

OHIO UNIVERSITY LIBRARY

Please return this book as soon
have finished with
fine it must be retur
stamped below